Key Concepts
in
American History

Expansionism

Key Concepts in American History

Expansionism

Richard Sauers, Ph.D.

Jennifer L. Weber, Ph.D.
General Editor
University of Kansas

CHELSEA HOUSE PUBLISHERS
An imprint of Infobase Publishing

Key Concepts in American History: Expansionism

Copyright © 2010 by DWJ BOOKS LLC

DEVELOPED, DESIGNED, AND PRODUCED BY DWJ BOOKS LLC

Chelsea House
An imprint of Infobase Publishing
132 West 31st Street
New York NY 10001

Library of Congress Cataloging-in-Publication Data

Sauers, Richard Allen.
   Expansionism / Richard Sauers; general editor, Jennifer L. Weber.
       p. cm.—(Key concepts in American history)
   Includes bibliographical references and index.
   ISBN 978-1-60413-221-2 (hardcover)
1. United States—Territorial expansion—Encyclopedias, Juvenile. 2. West (U.S.)—History—Encyclopedias, Juvenile. 3. Frontier and pioneer life—West (U.S.)—Encyclopedias, Juvenile. I. Weber, Jennifer L., 1962– II. Title. III. Series.
   E179.5.S25 2010
   978′.02—dc22

                              2009029614

Chelsea House books are available at special discounts when purchased in bulk quantities for businesses, associations, institutions, or sales promotions. Please call our Special Sales Department in New York at (212) 967-8800 or (800) 322-8755.

You can find Chelsea House on the World Wide Web at http://www.chelseahouse.com

Cover printed by Bang Printing, Brainerd, MN
Book printed and bound by Bang Printing, Brainerd, MN
Date printed: May 2010
Printed in the United States of America

10 9 8 7 6 5 4 3 2 1

This book is printed on acid-free paper.

Acknowledgments
pp. 1, 25, 46, 54, 76: The Granger Collection, New York; pp. 14, 70, 94: Private Collection/Peter Newark Western Americana/The Bridgeman Art Library; pp. 39, 83: Private Collection/Peter Newark American Pictures/The Bridgeman Art Library.

Contents

Viewpoints About Expansionism

List of Illustrations

Reader's Guide
to Expansionism

The list that follows is provided as an aid to readers in locating articles on the big topics or themes of the **expansionist** period of American history. The Reader's Guide arranges all of the A to Z entries in *Key Concepts in American History: Expansionism* according to these **6 key concepts** of the social studies curriculum: **Economics and Trade; Explorers and Discoveries; Government and Policy; People and Society; Religion;** and **Wars and Battles.** Some articles appear in more than one category, helping readers to see the links between topics.

Economics and Trade
Alaska
American Samoa
California
California Gold Rush
Cuba
Filibustering Expeditions
Hawaii
Manifest Destiny
Native Americans
Oregon Country
Oregon Trail
Panama Canal
Pony Express
Santa Fe Trail
Slavery
Texas

Explorers and Discoveries
Alaska
American Samoa
Cuba
Hawaii
Lewis and Clark Expedition
Northern Mariana Islands
Philippines
Puerto Rico
Santa Fe Trail
Virgin Islands

Government and Policy
Cuba
Dollar Diplomacy
Filibustering Expeditions
Florida
Gadsden Purchase
Jackson, Andrew (see Native Americans)
Kansas-Nebraska Act
Louisiana Purchase
Manifest Destiny
Northern Mariana Islands
Panama Canal
Philippines
Polk, James K. (1795–1849)
Pony Express
Popular Sovereignty
Puerto Rico
Slavery
States, Admission of New
Texas
Wilmot Proviso

People and Society
Cass, Lewis (see Popular Sovereignty)
Dewey, Admiral George (see Philippines)
Douglas, Stephen A. (1813–1861)
Dred Scott Case
Filibustering Expeditions
Jackson, Andrew (see Native Americans)
Lincoln, Abraham (1809–1865)
Native Americans
Northern Mariana Islands
Pony Express

Queen Liliuokalani (see Hawaii)
Roosevelt, Theodore (see Spanish-American War)
Sacajawea (see Lewis and Clark Expedition)
Seward, William (1801–1872)
Slavery
Sutter, John (see California Gold Rush)
Tyler, John (1790–1862)
Webster-Ashburton Treaty
Whitman, Marcus and Narcissa (1802–1847, 1808–1847)

Religion
Hawaii
Philippines
Whitman, Marcus and Narcissa (1802–1847; 1808–1847)
Utah Territory

Wars and Battles
Cuba
Dewey, Admiral George (see Philippines)
Filibustering Expeditions
Mexican-American War (1846–1848)
Seminole War
Spanish-American War (1898)
Texas
Philippines

Milestones in

After the United States won its independence from Great Britain in 1783, many Americans believed that the nation would one day reach across the entire continent of North America. With the Louisiana Purchase of 1803, the nation began expanding westward. By 1854, the nation filled its present-day continental borders from east to west. Americans then sought to increase their influence, buying Alaska from Russia, annexing the Hawaiian Islands, and establishing a global empire after winning the Spanish-American War in 1898.

1783 Treaty of Paris establishes the Mississippi River as the western boundary of the United States.

1803 With the Louisiana Purchase, the United States doubles in size.

1821 Spanish Florida is annexed; Adams-Onís Treaty establishes border between the United States and Spanish Mexico.

1836 Texas gains independence from Mexico; Marcus and Narcissa Whitman establish a mission in the Oregon Country.

1841 William Henry Harrison is elected the ninth president of the United States but dies one month later; John Tyler (1841–1845) assumes the presidency.

1842 Webster-Ashburton Treaty establishes the boundary between Maine and British Canada.

1844 James K. Polk (1845–1849) is elected the 11th president of the United States.

1845 The United States annexes Texas.

1846 Mexican-American War begins.

1848 Mexican-American War ends; the United States gains a vast area known as the Mexican Cession.

1849 Gold is discovered in California.

1850 California is admitted to the Union.

1854 The United States acquires the Gadsden Purchase from Mexico, completing the boundaries of the continental United States; Republican Party is organized to oppose the spread of slavery to the territories.

1857 *Dred Scott* decision declares that African Americans are not citizens of the United States; further declares that the Missouri Compromise of 1820 was unconstitutional; the decision opens the possibility that slavery would spread to all the states.

1867 The United States purchases Alaska from Russia.

1896 Utah is admitted to the Union.

1898 Spanish-American War makes the United States an imperial power; the country acquires Cuba, Puerto Rico, Guam, and the Philippines; United States annexes Hawaii.

1901 President William McKinley (1897–1901) is assassinated;

Expansionism (1803–Present)

Theodore Roosevelt (1901–1909) assumes the presidency.

1902 The United States grants Cuba independence.

1903 Panama gains independence from Colombia.

1904 Construction begins on the Panama Canal.

1914 Panama Canal opens, greatly reducing the travel time between the eastern and western coasts of the United States.

1917 The United States purchases the Virgin Islands from Denmark.

1946 The United States grants the Philippines independence.

1947 Northern Mariana Islands become a part of the Trust Territory of the Pacific, administered by the United States.

1952 Residents of Puerto Rico become U.S. citizens.

1959 Alaska is admitted to the Union as the 49th state; Hawaii is admitted to the Union as the 50th state.

1972 Northern Mariana Islands become a territory of the United States.

1977 U.S. president Jimmy Carter (1977–1981) and Panamanian president Omar Torrijos agree to return control of the canal to Panama in 1999.

1986 Residents of the Northern Mariana Islands become citizens of the United States.

1998 Puerto Ricans vote on the island's status with the United States; vote is inconclusive, and Puerto Rico remains a Commonwealth.

1999 Panama assumes full control of the Panama Canal.

2009 Barack Obama (2009–) is inaugurated as the 44th president of the United States; Obama works to establish a new tone of cooperation with other nations and in October is awarded the Nobel Peace Prize.

Preface

The United States was founded on ideas. Those who wrote the U.S. Constitution were influenced by ideas that began in Europe: reason over religion, human rights over the rights of kings, and self-governance over tyranny. Ideas, and the arguments over them, have continued to shape the nation. Of all the ideas that influenced the nation's founding and its growth, 10 are perhaps the most important and are singled out here in an original series—KEY CONCEPTS IN AMERICAN HISTORY. The volumes bring these concepts to life, *Abolitionism, Colonialism, Expansionism, Federalism, Industrialism, Internationalism, Isolationism, Nationalism, Progressivism*, and *Terrorism*.

These books examine the big ideas, major events, and influential individuals that have helped define American history. Each book features three sections. The first is an overview of the concept, its historical context, the debates over the concept, and how it changed the history and growth of the United States. The second is an encyclopedic, A-to-Z treatment of the people, events, issues, and organizations that help to define the "-ism" under review. Here, readers will find detailed facts and vivid histories, along with referrals to other books for more details about the topic.

Interspersed throughout the entries are many high-interest features: "History Speaks" provides excerpts of documents, speeches, and letters from some of the most influential figures in American history. "History Makers" provides brief biographies of key people who dramatically influenced the country. "Then and Now" helps readers connect issues of the nation's past with present-day concerns.

In the third part of each volume, "Viewpoints," readers will find longer primary documents illustrating ideas that reflect a certain point of view of the time. Also included are important government documents and key Supreme Court decisions.

The KEY CONCEPTS series also features "Milestones in. . . ," time lines that will enable readers to quickly sort out how one event led to another, a glossary, and a bibliography for further reading.

People make decisions that determine history, and Americans have generated and refined the ideas that have determined U.S. history. With an understanding of the most important concepts that have shaped our past, readers can gain a better idea of what has shaped our present.

Jennifer L. Weber, Ph.D.

Assistant Professor of History, University of Kansas

General Editor

What Is Expansionism?

Expansionism is the process of growth through the acquisitions—either by purchase or by warfare—of a nation. Understanding the theme of expansionism is essential to learning how and why the United States grew geographically and economically since colonial times.

In fewer than 100 years, the United States grew from a union of 13 former English **colonies** to a continental power, one that stretched from the Atlantic Ocean westward to the Pacific. In the 30 years after expanding from sea to sea, the United States became a world power following a brief war with Spain and the acquisition of the Spanish possessions of Guam, the Philippines, Cuba, and Puerto Rico. By the end of World War I (1914–1918), the United States had completed a canal across the **Isthmus** of Panama and acquired yet another Caribbean possession—the U.S. Virgin Islands.

The United States was not the only major country that grew across a continent. Between the 1500s and 1700s, Russia had expanded eastward from Europe across the Ural Mountains and Siberia to the Pacific Ocean. Canada, too, grew from the Atlantic to the Pacific during the 1800s. American expansion, though, differed from these other nations in several ways.

Secretary of State William H. Seward (seated, left) was an enthusiastic supporter of U.S. expansionism. In this painting, he oversees the signing on March 30, 1867, of the Alaska Purchase Agreement which finalized the purchase from Russia for $7.2 million. The U.S. minister to Russia, Edouard de Stoeckel, points to Alaska on the globe.

A SENSE OF MISSION

Ever since the first European settlers arrived on the east coast of the North American continent, a sense of divine mission existed in the early colonies, especially in New England. Puritans from England felt that they had been sent by God to establish a new society. The city of Boston, in the Massachusetts colony, was described as a beacon on a hill to light the world. A new life in the Americas would allow the settlers and their religion to flourish without persecution.

Although not all **immigrants** to early America had this thought, there evolved over time an idea that the United States was different from the older European countries from which most Americans had come. By the 1840s, this sense of mission came to be called "manifest destiny," the belief that America's mission was to occupy the North American continent and spread **democracy** across the land. Some historians have called this idea "democratic imperialism," because Americans of the nineteenth century believed it was their duty to "civilize" those peoples less fortunate than themselves. In the view of those who believed in manifest destiny, America's abundant natural resources, its growing population, and vast expanse of land meant that God had favored the American people, who in turn believed they must take advantage of these sacred gifts and expand.

NATIVE AMERICANS

This sense of mission also contained strands of **racism.** Manifest destiny was only for white people. In general, everybody else was considered inferior to the sturdy young pioneers moving westward across the continent. Open warfare between colonists and Native Americans quickly erupted as more and more settlers pushed westward and threatened native tribes and their homelands.

Negotiation and Relocation While many American leaders tried to negotiate **treaties** with the native peoples, there were always more settlers willing to ignore such treaties as they moved west to locate better land on which to build their homes. Treaty after treaty was broken by one side or the other as settlers pushed west. By the late 1820s, the American government, with Andrew Jackson (1829–1837) as president, advocated Indian removal as a way of preventing bloodshed.

Under this policy of relocation, the government negotiated buyouts of Native American tribal land east of the Mississippi River and forced the eastern tribes to **emigrate** from their lands and immigrate to selected areas west of the river, mostly to present-day Oklahoma. The most horrific of these forced relocations, which occurred in the 1830s, is known as the "Trail of Tears." It was thought that Native Americans would be left alone as their culture developed to a point where they could be assimilated into American society in the future.

Further Restrictions The rapid westward advance of white civilization, however, constantly threatened the lifestyles of the Native American tribes. The discovery of gold in California in 1848 led to a sudden rush of **prospectors** across the Great Plains and Rocky Mountains to the West Coast. The Plains tribes fought white encroachment for decades until forced onto **reservations** by the end of the 1880s, when organized warfare ceased.

EXPANSION, 1783–1861

The peace treaty ending the Revolutionary War (1775–1783) was extremely favorable to the United States. As a result of the Seven Years' War, also known as the French and Indian War, (1754–1763), King George III (1760–1820) had forbidden colonial settlement west of the Appalachian Mountains so as not to provoke Native American attacks. By the end of the revolution, few American settlers had crossed the Appalachians in defiance of the king's decree. Still, American negotiators at the peace conference in Paris wanted the region west of the Appalachians and refused to give up this vast area. Thus, instead of being confined to the eastern seaboard, the new United States totaled around 900,000 square miles (233,098,929.93 hectares), 70 percent of which was west of the Appalachians. At the time, the population of the new nation was only about 4 million people, including enslaved Africans.

The young United States was surrounded by enemy powers, with the British to the north in Canada and the Spanish to the west and south. Although Spain had aided the colonists during their revolt from Great Britain, the Spanish monarchy worried about the young democracy in the Americas and its possible effects on their own colonies in the hemisphere. Native Americans and fugitive slaves ran into Spanish territory to avoid pursuit. New Orleans, the major port on the Mississippi River, was owned by the Spanish, who strictly regulated U.S. trade coming down the river.

Expansion West of the Mississippi When Napoleon of France acquired the Louisiana Territory from Spain in the early 1800s, he hoped to build a new French empire in North America. However, realizing that his forces could not compete with the British Royal Navy, together with a failed attempt to suppress a slave revolt in French-ruled Haiti, Napoleon decided to sell Louisiana to the United States in 1803. The Louisiana Purchase doubled the size of the United States and gave the Americans control of the Mississippi River.

The vague western and northern boundaries of the Louisiana Purchase led to disagreements with both Spain and Great Britain. American and British negotiators settled the northern boundary in 1818. After the Spanish government realized that it was too weak to prevent American raids into Florida after hostile Native Americans, Spain and the United States reached an agreement in 1819 under which Spain ceded Florida to the United States and settled the western boundary of the Louisiana Purchase.

Further Expansion Boundaries on a map, however, did little to stop American expansion. The quest for cheap land led thousands of Americans into Spanish Mexico in the 1820s and 1830s. Even after Mexican independence from Spain in 1821, lax regulation of existing laws meant that Americans soon outnumbered Mexicans in the province of Texas. Later, when the Mexican government tried to enforce its laws in the province, Texas revolted in 1835 and became independent in 1836. Many Texans wished that the United States would **annex** the Lone Star Republic, but political disagreement in Washington, D.C.—primarily over slavery—prevented annexation from taking place until 1845.

When annexation did take place, it led to war with Mexico (1846–1848) that President James K. Polk (1845–1849) was eager to start. Polk, an enthusiastic supporter of manifest destiny, had wanted to take control of California, and the war with Mexico gave him the opportunity to do so. The peace treaty ending the war gave the United States the Mexican provinces of California and New Mexico. Together with the settlement of the Oregon Territory boundary with Great Britain, the United States now stretched from coast to coast.

TERRITORIES AND STATES

Expansion meant the acquisition of new land. Congress passed the Land Ordinance of 1785 to make expansion orderly into the territory west of the Appalachians, land that had been acquired as a result of the 1783 Treaty of Paris.

In 1787, Congress passed the Northwest Ordinance to better organize the territory north of the Ohio River. This law provided that this region would be divided into three to five territories. Each territory would have a governor, secretary, and three judges, all appointed by Congress. When a territory's population reached 5,000 adult males, it would be allowed an elected assembly. When there were 60,000 inhabitants, the territory could apply to Congress to become a state on equal footing with the original 13 states. Slavery was prohibited in these new territories.

Applying the Laws in the New Lands Congress eventually extended the statehood principal—as outlined in the ordinances of 1785 and 1787—to all continental territory that was acquired by the United States. By doing so, potential revolts were eliminated because, when it grew to the proper number of people, a territory could be given statehood. Settlers continued to have all the rights of American citizens, another important reason that revolts never threatened territorial stability.

EXPANSION AND SLAVERY

As the United States expanded westward, the slavery issue became embedded in territorial arguments. Although the Constitution allowed and even protected slavery, by the early 1800s an **abolition** movement was growing across the North. Most Northern states had gradually **emancipated** their slaves and prohibited any human bondage. The Northwest Ordinance prohibited slavery in the Northwest Territory and in any states formed (Ohio, Indiana, Illinois, Michigan, and part of Minnesota) from that territory.

The Missouri Compromise When Missouri petitioned to become a state in 1819, the slavery issue was brought before Congress. Northern attacks on the immorality of slavery had grown, convincing many Southerners who did not own slaves to unite with slave owners in order to defend their unique Southern way of life. The Missouri Compromise of 1820 settled temporarily the issue of slavery in the territories. However, the Mexican War brought up the question of slavery again. Many Northerners believed that the war was simply a plot by slaveholders to extend the institution, and they refused to support the conflict.

The Compromise of 1850 The Compromise of 1850 again tried to solve the slavery issue politically. Under this compromise, California was admitted to the Union as a free state, and the settlers of the Utah and New Mexico territories would be allowed to decide whether to allow slavery. Later, Democratic senator Stephen A. Douglas of Illinois, however, advocated the idea of popular sovereignty, which would allow the residents of each territory to decide whether or not to have slavery. This idea set off a storm of protest across the North.

In 1854, opponents of slavery founded the Republican Party to stop the spread of slavery into the new territories. Open warfare between proslavery and antislavery settlers erupted in the Kansas Territory in 1856 and continued until 1861. By 1856, the slavery issue had entered presidential politics when Democrat James Buchanan won a heated electoral contest over Republican John C. Frémont. Four years later, in 1860, Republican Abraham Lincoln (1861–1865) was elected to the presidency because the Democratic Party itself split over the slavery issue.

POST–CIVIL WAR EXPANSION

The Civil War (1861–1865) halted American expansion, but in 1867, the United States acquired the Alaska Territory from Russia. The war also temporarily disrupted the nation's economic growth. Yet, spurred by a tremendous expansion of railroads and the effects of the 1862 Homestead Act, which gave away western land in return for living on the land for five years and improving it, westward settlement greatly expanded after 1865. The government had by this time decided that it was easier to give land away rather than sell it for profit. So, to encourage railroad growth, the government gave generous land grants to railroad companies.

Economic historians note that the American economy matured in the late 1880s and early 1890s. The growing population was now augmented by a wave of **immigration** from eastern and southern Europe that provided new employees for factories and businesses. Agriculture was expanding, as were American exports. Even the financial crisis known as the Panic of 1893 only put a temporary damper on the rising economy.

This "New Manifest Destiny" was propelled in part by Captain Alfred Thayer Mahan, a Naval War College professor who in 1890 published *The Influence of Sea Power Upon History, 1660–1783*. In this groundbreaking book, Mahan wrote about how sea power influenced national expansion. A growing nation needed an expanding foreign commerce to ensure national prosperity. Therefore, a nation needed a large **merchant marine** to keep foreign shipping from taking profits away. Overseas colonies and a strong navy would keep the merchant shipping safe and prosperous. Because the United States did not have overseas colonies, Mahan wrote that a powerful American navy was needed to keep American ports safe for foreign ships in case of war and to prevent enemy warships from attacking the American coasts.

THE SPANISH-AMERICAN WAR

Eight years after Mahan's *Influence of Sea Power* appeared, the United States went to war with Spain. Spain's harsh rule in Cuba was largely responsible for the war. American interest in Cuba began long before the Civil War, when Southern expansionists wanted the island to extend slavery. A reluctant President William McKinley (1897–1901) sent a war message to Congress in April 1898; by August, the fighting was over. The resulting peace treaty gave Puerto Rico, Cuba, and Guam to the United States, which also bought the Philippine Islands for $20 million. Cuba would eventually become independent, as would the Philippines. The Hawaiian Islands were also annexed during the Spanish-American War.

The United States suddenly had become a colonial power. The Spanish-American War had also demonstrated the need for a canal across Central America. President Theodore Roosevelt (1901–1909) quickly recognized the new nation of Panama when it revolted from Colombia, and he secured a treaty allowing the United States to build a canal, which opened in 1914. Purchase of the Danish Virgin Islands by the United States during World War I (1914–1918) completed U.S. overseas possessions.

EXPANSIONISM TODAY

Today, the United States retains Puerto Rico, the U.S. Virgin Islands, Guam, American Samoa, and the Northern Mariana Islands. The United States also owns several very small islands in the Pacific Ocean– Canton, Enderbury, Howland, Baker, Jarvis, Palmyra, Wake, Johnston, Sand, Kingman Reef, and Midway. In the Caribbean, the United States owns Navassa, a tiny isle between Jamaica and Haiti.

FURTHER READING

Kluger, Richard. *Seizing Destiny: How America Grew from Sea to Shining Sea*. New York: Alfred A. Knopf, 2007.

Nugent, Walter. *Habits of Empire: A History of American Expansion*. New York: Alfred A. Knopf, 2008.

A

Alaska

Russian North American territory sold to the United States in 1867, a bargain at the time which has proven to be of great importance to the United States. A Danish seafarer named Vitus Bering who was employed by Russia discovered modern Alaska in 1741. Russian interest in the cold, snow-covered land was very slow to develop. Alaska was thousands of miles from St. Petersburg, the Russian capital. Travel and communications took many months. **Indigenous** Alaskan tribes also objected to Russians trespassing on their land.

As a result, Russian **colonization** of Alaska was always minimal. Russian commercial interest in obtaining the pelts of sea otters was the principal motive that brought about the formation of the Russian American Company in 1799. This company was the consolidation of smaller companies operating in Alaska to harvest sea otters and sell the pelts, which were highly prized in European fashion. Backed by the Russian government, the company maintained a monopoly, forbidding trade in Alaska by non-Russians. The center of Russian settlement in Alaska was the town of New Archangel (present-day Sitka) on Baranov Island. Tense relations with the Tlingit tribe prevented any aggressive Russian expansion.

In addition to claims in Alaska, the Russian government also attempted to establish colonies as far south as present-day northern California. American settlement in the Oregon Territory and the westward expansion of the British Hudson's Bay Company, however, led to treaties in 1821 and 1824 that defined the borders of Russian Alaska. By that time, fashion had changed, and otter fur was no longer in demand. The Russian government, tired of providing money to keep the Russian American Company afloat, began to think about selling Alaska. The Crimean War (1853–1856)—in which Russia fought against the forces of Great Britain, France, the Ottoman Empire, and the Kingdom of Sardinia—showed Russia that it would be impossible to defend Alaska from a British attack from Canada in case of a future war.

Czar Alexander II (1855–1881) made the decision to sell Alaska in 1857. Edouard de Stoeckl, the Russian ambassador in Washington, approached the U.S. government about a deal. President James Buchanan (1857–1861) was interested, but the slavery issue preoccupied that nation and put any purchase on hold. Stoeckl later opened talks with the administration of Andrew Johnson (1865–1869) in early 1867. Secretary of State William H. Seward was an enthusiastic supporter of American expansion. He firmly believed that the United States would eventually occupy the entire North American continent, absorbing both Mexico and Canada in the process.

In order not to appear weak to his people, Alexander II instructed Stoeckl that any initial negotiations about Alaska must seem to come from the American side. Seward offered $5 million for Alaska. He then sought permission from the Senate to up the offer to $7.2 million. By March 29, 1867, both sides had agreed to this figure.

Seward went to see Senator Charles Sumner of Massachusetts, chairman of the Foreign Relations Committee and one of the most powerful Republicans in Washington. Seward managed to convince Sumner that acquiring Alaska was an important step for the United States. Sumner in turn steered the treaty through his committee before presenting it to the full Senate for consideration.

Sumner's three-hour speech to the full Senate included five advantages to the United States when it acquired Alaska: commercial opportunities for the West Coast, extension of American territorial domain, the extension of American republican institutions to Alaska, prevention of British influence in Alaska, and

a closer relationship with Russia. The Senate approved the purchase of Alaska by a vote of 37–2. The House of Representatives, which approved any funds for such treaties, eventually voted in favor, 114–43, in July 1868.

On October 18, 1867, the Russian flag was lowered at Sitka and replaced by the Stars and Stripes. The United States had acquired a territory that measured 586,400 square miles (151,876,902 hectares) for $7.2 million, a price of 2.5 cents an acre. Critics called it "Seward's Folly" and "Seward's Icebox." Indeed, there were perhaps only 900 Russians and Americans in Alaska in 1867, with another 30,000 Native Americans.

Alaska was ignored by the U.S. government for decades. The new territory was run by the army and provided little **revenue** for the United States. However, repeated discoveries of gold at Juneau (1880), Klondike (1896), Nome (1898), and Fairbanks (1902) led to gold rushes similar to the 1840s California gold rush. Oil was discovered as early as 1902, but the major discovery took place in 1968 on the North Slope, revealing the largest oil field in North America. Alaska became a territory in 1912 and, finally, the 49th state in 1959.

FURTHER READING

Alaska A to Z. Bellevue, Wash.: Vernon Publications, 1993.

Madden, Ryan. *Alaska* (On the Road Histories). Northampton, Mass.: Interlink Publishing Group, 2005.

American Samoa

Group of islands in the South Pacific occupied by the United States in the late nineteenth century. The Samoan Islands are roughly halfway between Hawaii and Australia. The islands together amount only to about 76 square miles (19,683 hectares), about the same size as the District of Columbia. The islands are tropical and receive about 200 inches (508 cm) of rain each year.

A Dutch navigator was the first European to see the islands in 1722. French and British explorers followed and established **missions** on several islands, most notably Tutuila, the largest Samoan island.

The first American to visit Samoa was Lieutenant Charles Wilkes of the U.S. Navy; Wilkes was leading a scientific expedition across the Pacific. The lieutenant visited Tutuila in 1839 and noted that the village of Pago Pago (pronounced Pango Pango) on the island's southern shore had an excellent deepwater harbor.

As American commerce expanded in the Pacific after the Civil War (1861–1865), traders and other business leaders began to realize that Samoa could furnish an important **coaling station** for their ships. In 1872, Navy Commander Richard Meade negotiated a treaty with local chiefs that gave the United States exclusive rights to use the harbor as a coaling station. The chiefs also gave the United States the right to negotiate any disputes with European nations that might occur in Samoa.

Shortly after American interest in Samoa began to grow, British and German merchants started to arrive. Interested in acquiring the exclusive right to **export** coconut oil from Samoa, Germany insisted that it take full control over the islands. President Grover Cleveland's (1885–1889, 1893–1897) administration confronted Germany by sending a squadron of warships to Samoa. Great Britain did the same, and for a brief time, it appeared that a war among the three powers over control of Samoa might erupt. However, a tropical hurricane inflicted great damage on the fleets and forced a resolution of the Samoan question. All three nations agreed to jointly protect the islands.

Ten years later, in 1899, due to continued conflict between the powers, Samoa was divided between Germany and the United States. The United States took possession of the eastern islands, which included Tutuila, while Germany received the western islands; Great Britain opted out of the agreement. During World War I (1914–1918), New Zealand took control of the German half of Samoa, then administered the islands as a United Nations **Trust Territory** until 1962, when Western Samoa became independent.

The U.S. Navy was awarded administrative control of American Samoa, which became an important naval base during the early years of World War II (1939–1945). The Department of the Interior, which is responsible for public land, was given jurisdiction over the islands in 1951. In 1954, Van Camp Seafood Company opened a tuna cannery in Samoa, followed shortly thereafter by Starkist.

Canned tuna has become a mainstay of the island economy, as has tourism. Since 1977, the territorial governor has been elected by Samoans; the land remains an American territory thousands of miles from the mainland United States.

FURTHER READING

American Samoa: 100 Years Under the United States Flag. N.p.: Island Heritage, 2000.

American Samoa Historic Preservation Office. Available online. URL: *http://www.ashpo.org*

Bennet, Michelle. *Lonely Planet Samoan Islands*. Oakland, Calif.: Lonely Planet Publications, 2003.

C–D

California

Northernmost region of the Pacific coast province of Mexico that was **ceded** to the United States in 1848; Spanish explorers had claimed California in 1542, after which Spanish culture, along with Roman Catholicism, slowly moved into the area by way of **missions** set up by the Catholic Church to "civilize" Native Americans living in the area.

Mexican independence in the 1820s, however, led to a decline in the missions as well as a loosening of any influence from the new capital of Mexico City, more than 1,500 miles (2,414 km) from Los Angeles. By the late 1830s, the Mexican province of California was a **de facto** independent entity of Mexico, with a feuding governor in Los Angeles and military commander in Monterey.

HIDDEN AGENDAS

After James K. Polk (1845–1849) was inaugurated as president of the United States in 1845, he was instrumental in settling the controversy over the boundary of the Oregon Territory and in provoking a war with Mexico over the southern boundary of Texas. Polk also had a hidden agenda in acquiring California by purchase or force, whichever would work. Polk worried that Great Britain, which had shown an interest in California, might take control of the area. Therefore, the president decided that the United States had to have California to complete its territorial march across North America.

The Mexican-American War (1846–1848) began in May 1846. Captain John C. Frémont quickly rode southward from Oregon into California, but instead of allowing the locals to declare their own independence, Frémont's men rode into Sonoma and declared an independent "Bear Flag Republic" on June 14, so named after the grizzly bear emblem on a homemade flag.

MILITARY MOVEMENTS

In addition to Frémont, the U.S. diplomat at Monterey, Thomas O. Larkin, was also working undercover for the State Department and helped foment rebellion. Aided by the American Pacific Squadron, Frémont had northern California under his control by July. Commodore Robert Stockton brought a contingent of U.S. Marines and sailors ashore to help Frémont's growing force of volunteers. By mid-

August, his troops had moved south and occupied San Diego, Los Angeles, and Santa Barbara.

AMERICANS TAKE CONTROL

The Treaty of Guadalupe-Hidalgo (1848), which ended the Mexican War, awarded the province of California to the United States. America acquired a province that was yet largely unknown to most outsiders. What *was* known was the excellent harbor at the town of Yerba Buena, which was renamed San Francisco in January 1847. This large harbor was the only one on the Pacific coast south of Puget Sound (on the northeastern coast of Washington State) that did not front directly on the ocean, thus creating a perfect anchorage for ships.

See also: Mexican-American War; Polk, James K.

FURTHER READING

Harlow, Neal. *California Conquered: The Annexation of a Mexican Province, 1846–1850.* Berkeley: University of California Press, 1989.

Kluger, Richard. *Seizing Destiny: How America Grew from Sea to Shining Sea.* New York: Alfred A. Knopf, 2007.

California Gold Rush

Precious metal discovery that led to a frenzied rush to mine gold in California in the late 1840s, giving California international recognition and leading to quick settlement of the area. Thus, by 1850, California asked to join the Union as the 31st state and continue the nation's expansion westward.

Although Spain had claimed California in 1542, the province had never been developed because of its distance from Mexico City, then the capital of New Spain. California authorities **exported** cattle products as the province's main source of income. They also granted extensive land holdings to **immigrant** settlers in hopes of building up the local economy.

IMMIGRANTS IN CALIFORNIA

One such newcomer was John Sutter, a Swiss immigrant who came to California by way of the United States. Sutter arrived in California in 1839 and was granted permission to settle in the province's lush Central Valley, northeast of the small settlement of San Francisco. Sutter chose a location where the Sacramento and American rivers meet, in the midst of the Sacramento Valley, located between the coastal mountains and the towering Sierra Nevada to the east.

GOLD IS DISCOVERED

In the summer of 1847, Sutter sent carpenter James W. Marshall 40 miles (64 km) upstream along the South Fork of the American River to construct a sawmill. On January 24, 1848, Marshall discovered small pieces of gold in the mill's tailrace, below the waterwheel. He reported his find to Sutter, who tried to keep it quiet, but word soon reached San Francisco, 100 miles (161 km) to the southwest, thanks to a local store owner who realized that gold miners coming to the area would need supplies.

San Francisco quickly emptied of men as word spread about the gold find. Soon, miners were combing the streams flowing out of the Sierra

A prospector uses a sluice box on the banks of a California river as he searches for gold. Looking for gold was difficult, backbreaking work, and only a few lucky miners became wealthy for their effort.

Nevada, hoping to find gold. Sutter lost much of his land to **prospectors** who flooded into the area. The small city of Sacramento grew as thousands of men headed to the gold fields. California had become an American possession at the end of the Mexican War (1846–1848), and the sudden influx of miners meant chaos for U.S. officials trying to keep order and sort out land claims. Colonel Richard Mason was unable to control conflicting land claims, noting:

"Upon considering the large extent of the country, the character of the people engaged and the small, scattered force at my command, I resolved not to interfere but to permit all to work freely."

THE GOLD RUSH

The worst was yet to come. Word slowly filtered back East, and when President James K. Polk (1845–1849) spoke about the discovery in his farewell address, gold fever gripped the

United States. Men left their families and employment and headed west in hopes of striking it rich.

Travel by Sea Many of those from the eastern seaboard states went by sea. Some vessels steamed south to Central America, where passengers left the ships, crossed through the rainforest to the Pacific coast, and embarked north to California. Other ships braved the passage around Cape Horn at the tip of South America and up the West Coast to San Francisco, a journey of six to eight months. Clipper ships cut the passage to 133 days but at peril of the weather around Cape Horn.

Travel by Land Americans from the Upper South and Midwest often traveled overland to California. Companies of men assembled along the western frontier in towns such as St. Joseph and Independence, Missouri, and Council Bluffs, Iowa. After outfitting themselves with equipment and arms, wagon trains set out along the Oregon Trail, across the Great Plains and the Rocky Mountains to Utah, where two trails branched off. The California Trail crossed the Sierra Nevada to Sutter's Fort. Others took the Santa Fe Trail, which ended up in San Diego. These "'49ers," which included eager prospectors from the United States, Mexico, South America, Asia, and Europe, came by the thousands both by land and sea, eager to find gold.

LOOKING FOR GOLD

Although an extremely lucky miner could accumulate thousands of dollars worth of gold dust and nuggets, such instances of striking it rich were rare. Early miners simply panned for gold, swishing gravel and sand around in a tin pan partly filled with water. Gold is heavy and sank to the bottom as the miner swished out the sand and gravel. This type of gold is called "placer gold," flecks of yellow metal mixed in with sand and gravel along the bottom of creeks and rivers. It was backbreaking work, the men standing for hours in ice-cold water while using their pans. "Lode gold" was mined from veins of quartz and other rock that contained gold. This mining required digging tunnels and blasting with dynamite.

As thousands of miners converged on the Sierra Nevada foothills, some of them brought or built better equipment to separate the gold. These devices included rockers (which resembled cradles and used a rocking motion to swish the water and gravel) and long toms (essentially long, wooden troughs with fine netting at the end to separate out the gold). These devices worked better with teams of men. Finally, hydraulic mining was used. A miner aimed a high-pressure hose to literally blast a riverbank of gravel apart, sending mud into a **sluice** to separate out the gold. This method was extremely detrimental to the environment and was outlawed in 1884.

Most gold miners went away disappointed. Although some miners could gather thousands of dollars worth of gold per day, most did not. Miners paid high prices for supplies in the camps and towns; all supplies had to be brought in by ship or overland at a high cost. Miners generally lived by their own code of law that meted out harsh punishment to

claim jumpers and thieves. Only when roads were built and towns grew did women and children come to the region to be with their men.

RESULTS

In the end, the gold rush brought California to national and international prominence as miners came from all over the world to pan for gold. Thousands of Chinese immigrants rushed to California, starting the Chinese community that still exists in the state. The sudden influx of inhabitants meant quick statehood (1850) for California, which bypassed the territory phase. Today, California still produces enough gold to place fourth among the other states (after South Dakota, Utah, and Alaska).

See also: California.

FURTHER READING

Andrist, Ralph K. *The California Gold Rush.* New York: American Heritage Publishing Company, 1961.

Mercati, Cynthia. *Forty-niners: The Story of the California Gold Rush.* Logan, Iowa: Perfection Learning, 2002.

Raum, Elizabeth. *The California Gold Rush: An Interactive History Adventure.* Mankato, Minn.: Capstone Press, 2008.

Sonneborn, Liz. *The California Gold Rush: Transforming the American West.* New York: Chelsea House, 2008.

Cass, Lewis

See Popular Sovereignty.

Cuba

Caribbean island owned by Spain since its discovery in 1492 until 1899, when the United States assumed a **protectorate** over the island.

Ever since the early 1800s, prominent Americans thought that the United States should acquire Cuba. The island was only 90 miles (145 km) from the southern tip of Florida and was a major **exporter** of sugar and an **importer** of American goods. Four U.S. presidents—Thomas Jefferson (1801–1809), James K. Polk (1845–1849), Franklin Pierce (1853–1857), and James Buchanan (1857–1861)—offered money to Spain for Cuba.

CONTINUED CALL FOR ANNEXATION

After the American Civil War (1861–1865), slavery in the United States ended, but expansionists continued to cry that Cuba should be under U.S. influence. Spanish rule in Cuba was harsh. Cubans revolted from 1868 to 1878, and again starting in 1895. This second revolt endangered the stability of American business interests in Cuba and President William McKinley (1897–1901) was besieged by requests that he intervene in the fighting.

Reluctantly, McKinley asked Congress to declare war on Spain in April 1898, after Spain had rebuffed American offers to **mediate** the conflict. When Congress declared war, Colorado Republican senator Henry M. Teller added an amendment whereby "the United States hereby disclaims any disposition or intention to exercise sovereignty, jurisdiction, or control over [Cuba] except for the pacification thereof, and asserts its determination, when that is accomplished, to leave the government and control of the Island to its people."

The Teller Amendment passed without a single dissenting vote.

Once the Spanish-American War (1898) was over, U.S. troops occupied Cuba until 1902. Under their supervision, roads and railroads were constructed, sugar and tobacco plantations were restructured, other industries such as copper mines and cigar factories were modernized, and peace was maintained. The annual threat of **yellow fever** was also greatly reduced. All this was done with an immense flow of American money to the island. Investors bought large chunks of Cuban real estate and pushed aside the poor, largely illiterate peasants who comprised much of Cuba's 1.5 million population.

MOVING TOWARD INDEPENDENCE

Cubans held an election in June 1900. Those who voted rejected the idea that Cuba be annexed to the United States. In 1901, President McKinley asked Cuban leaders to write a constitution based on that of the United States as a prelude to complete independence. Earlier that year, Republican senator Orville Platt of Connecticut sponsored an amendment to an army funding bill. The amendment had actually been written by Secretary of War Elihu Root. It stipulated that an independent Cuba could not make **treaties** with any other nation without American approval. Cuba also had to agree to allow the United States to intervene in any situation that would threaten Cuban independence, and to allow the United States to obtain land necessary for a naval base. Guantánamo Bay remains today a U.S. base on the island of Cuba.

Under pressure to accept the Platt Amendment, the Cuban legislature had no choice but to agree to it. As a result, Cuba became independent on May 20, 1902, when its first president, Tomás Estrada Palma, took the oath of office. President Palma received his salary from Washington, as well as instructions on how to govern and keep the United States happy.

Puppet Governments Palma was but the first in a line of puppet governments controlled by the United States. The old Spanish political system in Cuba included much corruption and bribery. American attempts to provide a democratic government clashed with this centuries-old system, and it largely failed. Most Cuban presidents were corrupt, and the island remained under American influence. American military forces occasionally had to intervene to restore order and maintain American economic influence. Troops were in Cuba from 1906 to 1909, in 1912, and from 1917 to 1922. In 1934, the U.S. Congress repealed the Platt Amendment and allowed Cuba greater freedom. The United States also signed a reciprocal trade agreement with Cuba, giving the United States domination over the Cuban economy.

General Fulgencio Batista had come to power in 1931 and controlled Cuban presidents from behind the scenes until he was elected president in 1940, serving until 1944, after which he retired to Florida. Batista staged a **coup** in 1952 and returned to Cuba, supervising an increasingly corrupt regime until ousted from power by revolutionary Fidel Castro in late 1958.

See also: Spanish-American War.

FURTHER READING

Baker, Christopher P. *Cuba Handbook*. Chico, Calif.: Moon Publications, 2006.

Dosal, Paul J. *A Brief History of Cuba*. Wheeling, Ill.: Harlan Davidson Publishing, 2006.

Staten, Clifford L. *The History of Cuba*. New York: Palgrave Macmillan, 2005.

Dewey, Admiral George

See Philippines.

Dollar Diplomacy

Early twentieth-century American policy that served to assist American bankers and investors in foreign countries. Dollar diplomacy was also an attempt to improve foreign relations with the nations in Latin America.

The fast expansion of American manufacturing in the decades after the Civil War (1861–1865) meant that there was always a surplus, or oversupply, that could be **exported** overseas. The expansion of the American banking system at this same time meant that millions of American dollars were available for investment in foreign countries.

BACKGROUND

President Theodore Roosevelt (1901–1909) was enthusiastic about expanding the United States' role as a great world power. Yet Roosevelt was also a realist and during his presidency conducted a foreign policy tailored to protect the nation's rising power. His greatest achievement while in office was the acquisition of land in Panama to construct a canal across the **isthmus** to facilitate both naval power and trade. Roosevelt worked hard to ensure a balance of power that would neutralize any potential threat to the United States.

William H. Taft (1909–1913) succeeded Roosevelt and chose Philander C. Knox as his secretary of state. Knox was a corporate lawyer who was eager to help advance American economic interests throughout the world. The booming American economy helped Knox's "spirited foreign commercial policy" that encouraged American investments abroad. Knox reorganized the State Department to provide close help to any American initiative that would benefit both the investors and the United States. This "dollar diplomacy" was not really a new foreign policy, but simply a more aggressive form of existing national policy.

THE CARIBBEAN

The main thrust of dollar diplomacy took place in the Caribbean. The ongoing construction of the Panama Canal was of utmost importance to the United States because it would ultimately provide the nation with a much shorter route from the East Coast to the West Coast. In addition, the Taft administration was concerned about the monetary problems of most Central American countries. Knox was interested in helping these countries form more stable governments that would build secure financial structures to prevent going into debt to European nations, a process that might lead to European military intervention to regain monetary losses.

The Dominican Republic The United States intervened in both the Dominican Republic and Haiti, which share the island of Hispaniola, just east of

U.S. Relations with Latin America

Political relations between the United States and the nations of Latin America have occupied a unique position in America's foreign policy. In 1823, the U.S. issued the Monroe Doctrine, warning European powers to stay out of the affairs of the Western hemisphere. During the early 1800s, some Latin American leaders, such as Simón Bolívar, wanted to strengthen hemispheric ties, even calling for a Pan-American conference in the late 1820s. Other Latin American leaders remained suspicious of their powerful neighbor to the north.

In the 1880s, U.S. Secretary of State James G. Blaine instituted the "Big Brother Policy." Blaine hoped to rally Latin American nations behind U.S. leadership and open new markets for the nation's growing industries. In 1889, Blaine arranged for the first Pan-American conference, much as had been envisioned by Bolívar years earlier. [Later, after World War II (1939–1945), these hemispheric conferences lead to the formation of the Organization of American States (OAS), which today meets to review issues and concerns among the nations of the Americas.]

In the late 1890s and early 1900s, relations between the U.S. and Latin America grew increasingly strained. Many Latin American nations believed that Cuba and Puerto Rico should have been granted immediate independence after the Spanish-American War (1898), rather than remaining under U.S. control. Furthermore, Latin American leaders were suspicious of the policies of President Theodore Roosevelt (1901–1909), who sought to extend U.S. political and economic influence in the region. President Roosevelt's policies were continued by his two successors, William H. Taft (1909–1913) and Woodrow Wilson (1913–1921).

Under the leadership of Franklin D. Roosevelt (1933–1945), policies toward Latin America changed. Roosevelt instituted the "Good Neighbor Policy," which sought to improve relations with Latin America. Under Roosevelt, the U.S. announced that it would not use its military to intervene in Latin American affairs.

Nonetheless, the U.S. stayed closely involved in Latin America. It supported puppet governments in many countries, immersed itself in Cuba's internal affairs, and in 1965, sent troops to the Dominican Republic to stop a leftist takeover of that nation's government. Throughout the 1970s and 1980s, the U.S. supported dictatorial Latin American regimes, especially if they were anti-Communist. After the fall of the Communist Soviet Union in 1991, the U.S. became less supportive of dictatorial government and encouraged the growth of democratically elected governments. In the early 2000s, however, many Latin American countries elected socialist governments; U.S. relations with these nations is sometimes strained as their leaders often embrace left-leaning policies, such as the nationalization of industries.

Cuba. Roosevelt had negotiated a treaty with the Dominican Republic in 1905, under which the United States appointed a **customs** supervisor who would use 55 percent of customs funds to pay off foreign creditors. The Dominican Republic agreed that it would not increase its foreign debt or raise taxes without U.S. approval. In effect, this treaty turned the Dominican Republic into an American **protectorate**.

In 1911, the Dominican Republic president was assassinated and several presidents held power briefly; these incompetent leaders gutted the national treasury to pay bribes in attempts to keep the army loyal. President Woodrow Wilson (1913–1921) finally decided to send a force of U.S. Marines to the Dominican Republic. The Marines landed on May 4, 1916, and eventually occupied the entire country. After another Dominican president refused to accept closer financial control by the United States, Wilson authorized that **martial law** be enacted in the Dominican Republic. Although the American occupation resulted in improved sanitation, roads, and other public works, it never promoted democratic stability, and the Marines withdrew in 1924. The United States continued to supervise the Dominican Republic's customs collection until 1940.

Haiti Haiti, independent since its revolt from France in 1804, also was a target of American dollar diplomacy. Haiti's population consisted primarily of uneducated peasants ruled by a small, elite class. Like the Dominican Republic, Haiti's poor economy meant that its rulers borrowed heavily from foreign bankers and went into debt, unable to repay loans. Between 1908 and 1915, seven different presidents (usually generals) ruled Haiti, which also saw at least 20 uprisings against those in power. In July 1915, President Vilbrun Guillaume Sam was overthrown and fled to the French embassy for safety. An angry crowd dragged him out and literally tore him to pieces.

This bloody revolt gave President Woodrow Wilson the excuse to intervene in an attempt to stabilize Haiti's government and prevent any European power from interfering. U.S. Marines landed on July 18, 1915, at Port-au-Prince, the capital city, seizing control of customhouses and other government offices. By the end of August, Marines controlled the entire country. A new Haitian president was nothing more than a **puppet** who cooperated with the Americans.

Final Withdrawal After crushing a revolt that took place between 1918 and 1920, American forces supervised the construction of new roads, wharves, and public buildings, including a new college and other schools. The Haitian president, however, refused to sign a loan agreement from the National City Bank of New York to repay existing loans. National City Bank, thanks to Secretary Knox's work in 1911, had become involved in Haiti's national bank and in 1917 took control of the bank.

In 1920, American officers replaced the Haitian president with

Louis Borno, who worked closely with the occupation forces to ensure that Haiti remained calm. U.S. forces finally left in 1934, when President Franklin D. Roosevelt (1933–1945) ordered them out. National City Bank sold its holdings to the Haitian national bank. American supervisors controlled Haiti's economy until its loan to the United States was paid off in 1947.

CENTRAL AMERICA

Most Central American nations were much like Haiti and the Dominican Republic—peasants ruled by a small, elite class. Countries such as Nicaragua, Guatemala, and Honduras endured revolt after revolt by military officers seeking to control their countries. Only Costa Rica remained peaceful. It was also the only country in the region that spent more money on education than on armed forces.

Political instability in many Central American countries and the protection of the Panama Canal were important concerns of the United States. Taft's secretary of state, Knox, said that his policy was "to make American capital the instrumentality to secure financial stability, and hence prosperity and peace, to the more backward republics in the neighborhood of the Panama Canal." American investment in Central America included banana companies, mines, shipping companies, and railroads. By the outbreak of World War I (1914–1918), the United States economically controlled much of Central America.

Therefore, when strongman José Zelaya of Nicaragua, an anti-American **dictator**, threatened the stability of neighboring countries, the United States eagerly supported a 1909 revolt against his rule. Zelaya was ousted from power, and when his supporters threatened the pro-American government, Knox in 1912 sent in the Marines to maintain law and order. The Marines remained until 1933. President Theodore Roosevelt had also sent Marines to Honduras in 1907 to stabilize that country's government, a friend of American-owned banana companies. Between 1911 and 1925, American troops intervened on six separate occasions in Honduras.

IMPACT OF DOLLAR DIPLOMACY

American dollar diplomacy was largely a failure. Thanks to the long-standing U.S. policy to support the 1823 Monroe Doctrine, which warned European powers to stay out the Western Hemisphere's affairs, U.S. presidents such as Theodore Roosevelt, Taft, and Wilson all worked toward that goal. By lending support to American bankers and investors hoping to secure commercial agreements in Central America and the Caribbean, the American government hoped to promote political stability and economic prosperity for poorer and unstable countries such as Nicaragua and Haiti. Protection for the Panama Canal was also behind many American interventions during the early twentieth century. In the end, while some interventions worked in America's favor, repeated military interventions on behalf of economics resulted in a rising anti-Americanism in Central and South America.

FURTHER READING

Foster, Lynn V. *A Brief History of Central America*. New York: Facts On File, 2000.

Rogozinski, Jan. *A Brief History of the Caribbean*. New York: Facts On File, 1999.

Veeser, Cyrus. *A World Safe for Capitalism: Dollar Diplomacy and America's Rise to Global Power*. New York: Columbia University Press, 2007.

Douglas, Stephen A. (1813–1861)

American politician most remembered for his 1858 senatorial debates and his 1860 presidential campaign against Abraham Lincoln (1861–1865). He was a major force in the Senate and made his biggest impact as chairman of the Committee on Territories. He was renowned as a great speaker and debater.

POLITICAL CAREER

In 1847, Douglas was elected to serve as a senator from Illinois. He was reelected twice.

As a member of the Senate, Douglas was greatly in favor of expanding the nation's borders. As a member of the Committee on Territories, Douglas was also involved in the heated debate over slavery in the new territories in the West. Douglas's first attempt at a solution was his support of popular sovereignty. Essentially, the people living in the territory would choose for themselves whether or not to allow slavery. This position, however, did not prove to be an acceptable solution.

In 1849, California sought to join the Union as a free state. Southern states protested because the balance of power in the U.S. Senate would then favor the free states. To maintain peace between North and South, Senator Henry Clay put together a series of proposals designed to appease both sides. After their initial failure, Senator Douglas shepherded these bills through the Senate. Known as the Compromise of 1850, the bills helped reach these compromises: California would be added as a free state. New Mexico and Utah would be allowed to decide the slave question for themselves. The Fugitive Slave Act of 1850 would require Northerners to assist in returning escaped slaves. In addition, Washington, D.C., would abolish its slave trade.

KANSAS-NEBRASKA ACT

The Compromise of 1850 quelled the slave debate for a while. It was reopened, however, by Douglas himself. In 1854, he pushed for the Kansas-Nebraska Act. Since 1820, slavery had been outlawed in the land north of the 36th parallel of the Louisiana Purchase. However, Douglas still believed in popular sovereignty—the idea that the people should decide whether to allow slavery——and the Kansas-Nebraska Act would allow the citizens of those future states to decide the slavery issue for themselves.

The act passed, a victory for Douglas, but the results were inflammatory and destructive. Antislavery and proslavery forces converged on Kansas, each attempting to sway the voters toward one side. This resulted in vicious fighting that became known as "Bleeding Kansas." The bloc of Southern states that had come together to pass the Kansas-Nebraska Act frightened Northern antislavery supporters, who feared the growing power of the slave states. In response, slavery opponents founded the Republican Party as a means to defend free states against Southern power. The Republican Party opposed the extension of slavery into the western territories.

1858 SENATE CAMPAIGN

In the 1858 senatorial election, Douglas famously engaged in a debate against Abraham Lincoln for Douglas's seat. The major point of contention was slavery. Douglas felt that settlers had the right to determine whether their state would allow slavery. Lincoln countered that the institution of slavery was ruining American government by creating "a house divided." He pointed out that slavery was dividing the country, turning the North and South into factions vying for control of the government. Douglas was reelected, but the debates made Lincoln a national figure.

1860 RUN FOR THE PRESIDENCY

Douglas failed to win 1860 presidential election in which he ran against Lincoln. When the Civil War (1861–1865) started, Douglas strongly supported the Union, denouncing the **secession** of the Southern states. He spent the last year of his life traveling in the border states trying to drum up support for the Union. He died of typhoid fever on June 3, 1861, in Chicago.

FURTHER READING

Huston, James L. *Stephen A. Douglas and the Dilemmas of Democratic Equality.* Lanham, Md.: Rowman & Littlefield Publishers, 2006.

Dred Scott *Case*

Controversial Supreme Court case that overturned the right of Congress to regulate slavery in the territories. The decision, an attempt to finally settle the question of slavery in newly acquired lands, resulted from the expansion of the United States after securing the Oregon Country and the Mexican Cession after the Mexican War (1846–1848).

Dred Scott was born enslaved in Virginia around 1795. His owner, Peter Blow, moved to St. Louis, Missouri, in 1827. After his master's death in 1831, Scott became the property of his daughter, Elizabeth. In 1833, he was sold to army doctor John Emerson.

Emerson was transferred from St. Louis to Rock Island, Illinois, in 1834. A year later, Dr. Emerson was sent to Fort Snelling, in present-day Minnesota. Emerson returned to St. Louis in 1838 and resided there until his death in 1844. Emerson's widow, Irene, moved to New York and left Dred Scott behind in Missouri with Henry Blow, a son of Scott's original owner.

THE FIRST COURT CASE

Henry Blow was an antislavery activist. In 1846, he financially backed a court case in Missouri to win Scott's freedom. Mrs. Emerson simply could have freed Scott, but she went along with the scheme and allowed herself to be sued for Scott's freedom. In the case *Dred Scott, a Man of Color, v. Emerson*, Scott's lawyers argued that because Scott had lived in free territory for several years, he was a free man and not a slave.

The lower court ruled in Scott's favor, but lawyers on the losing side appealed in an effort to get a ruling that would attract national attention to the issue of slavery in the territories. It took six years for the case to make its way through the Missouri courts. In 1852, the state supreme court ruled that since Scott had voluntarily returned to Missouri from free territory, he was still a slave.

THE SECOND CASE

In 1850, while the Missouri case was still pending, Mrs. Emerson married Dr. Calvin C. Chaffee, an **abolitionist** congressman from Massachusetts. Chaffee obviously was no slave owner and, like Mrs. Emerson earlier, could have freed Scott easily. Instead, Chaffee decided to again test Scott's freedom in federal court. To avoid being sued by Scott's lawyers, Chaffee "sold" Scott to Mrs. Emerson's brother, John F. A. Sanford of New York.

A Federal Case According to the Constitution, lawsuits brought by citizens of different states are tried in federal courts. Scott's lawyers brought the suit on behalf of their client, a citizen of Missouri. At the time, defenders of slavery argued that African Americans were not citizens and therefore had no legal rights. The federal circuit court accepted the case by ruling that Scott was indeed a Missouri citizen and had the right to sue in court. However, the court also ruled that Scott was still a slave.

Believing that their client was a free man, Scott's lawyers appealed the case to the U.S. Supreme Court. Both sides in this case wanted to get a ruling on the power of Congress to control the spread of slavery in the territories.

BEFORE THE SUPREME COURT

The case of *Dred Scott v. Sandford* (Sanford's name was misspelled by the court clerk) went before the Supreme Court in early 1856. After hearing arguments from both sides, the justices decided that the decision of the federal circuit court in Missouri should be upheld. In 1851, the court had decided that Kentucky slaves whose owner had allowed them to work in Ohio were still slaves because their rights were dependent on the state in which they resided. If the Supreme Court had simply announced this decision, it would have avoided any controversy about slavery in the territories.

A Dissenting Opinion However, Justice John McLean announced that he would write a dissenting opinion in which he would declare Scott a free man and uphold the right of Congress to legislate slavery in the territories. Massachusetts justice Benjamin R. Curtis concurred with McLean. The remaining seven members of the Court were all Democrats. Led by Chief Justice Roger Taney of Maryland, a former slave owner, the Court decided to delay action on the case until after the upcoming presidential election.

INTERFERENCE

Even after the presidential election, the Court continued to delay, partly because one justice was sick. Newspaper editors across the country wrote about the awaited ruling and how important it was for the country and the future of slavery. Congress was deadlocked over the issue of slavery in the Kansas Territory. Thus, president-elect James Buchanan (1857–1861) decided to see if he could learn in advance what the Court's decision would be. Buchanan knew that, after he was sworn into office on March 4, 1857, he would have to end the Kansas stalemate.

Buchanan wrote a private letter to Justice John Catron of Tennessee, a longtime friend, asking if the Court decision would occur before or after his inauguration. Catron replied that the decision would come in February. Even so, Catron continued, the decision would be restricted to the issue at hand, not slavery in the territories.

A painting of Dred Scott, taken from an 1858 photograph, shows the former slave shortly after he was freed. Scott was the subject of an 1857 landmark Supreme Court case in which it was declared that African Americans were not and could not become U.S. citizens. The ruling also declared the 1820 Missouri Compromise, which prohibited slavery in certain territories, to be unconstitutional.

As the time for the decision approached, Chief Justice Taney and other members of the Court decided to counteract the dissenting viewpoint by including a decision on the Missouri Compromise and the power of Congress over slavery. Buchanan was advised that the decision would not be handed down until after he became president. Therefore, during his inaugural speech, Buchanan proclaimed, "I shall cheerfully submit, whatever that [decision] shall be."

THE RULING

Chief Justice Taney delivered the Court's majority opinion two days after Buchanan, a Southern sympathizer from the North, became the nation's 15th president. Taney said that because African Americans were not citizens when both the Declaration of Independence and Constitution were written, they were at present not citizens. Therefore, as Scott was not a citizen, he had no right to use the court system, and thus his case was dismissed.

According to Taney, African Americans "had for more than a century been regarded as beings of an inferior order, and altogether unfit to associate with the white race, either in social or political relations; and so

History Speaks

Taney's Decision

Chief Justice Roger Taney wrote the majority opinion of the Supreme Court in *Dred Scott v. Sandford* (1857). Taney went into great detail attempting to show that the nation's Founders did not consider African Americans to be citizens of the United States. The following excerpt reveals some of Taney's reasoning that the Constitution clearly shows that there was a difference between white citizens and African American slaves. As a result, Taney believed African Americans could never become citizens.

It is true, every person, and every class and description of persons, who were at the time of the adoption of the Constitution recognized as citizens in the several States, became also citizens of this new political body; but none other; it was formed by them, and for them and their posterity, but for no one else. . . .

But there are two clauses in the Constitution which point directly and specifically to the negro race as a separate class of persons, and show clearly that they were not regarded as a portion of the people or citizens of the Government then formed. . . .

One of these clauses reserves to each of the thirteen States the right to import slaves until the year 1808 if he thinks it proper. And the importation which it thus sanctions was unquestionably of persons of the race of which we are speaking, as the traffic in slaves in the United States had always been confined to them. And by the other provision the States pledge themselves to each other to maintain the right of property of the master, by delivering up to him any slave who may have escaped from his service, and be found within their respective territories. . . . And these two provisions show, conclusively, that neither the description of persons therein referred to, nor their descendants, were embraced in any of the other provisions of the Constitution; for certainly these two clauses were not intended to confer on them or their posterity the blessings of liberty, or any of the personal rights so carefully provided for the citizen. . . .

far inferior, that they had no rights which the white man was bound to respect." No state had the right to expand the definition of citizenship to include free blacks because the **naturalization** process was reserved to Congress.

Taney went on to write that even if Scott had the right to sue in court, he would have lost his case. Just because he lived in a free state did not make Scott a free man. The Fifth Amendment to the Constitution states that no man can be deprived of his property without due process of law. Due to the terms of the Fifth Amendment, the Missouri Compromise was unconstitutional, as it prevented a man from taking his property north of Missouri without losing it. Congress could thus not keep slavery out of any U.S. territory, and neither could any territorial legislature.

Justices McLean and Benjamin R. Curtis delivered the dissenting opinion, declaring that Scott was a citizen and a free man. Curtis wrote that the Court did not have the right to rule on the Missouri Compromise after it had declared that Scott had no right to sue in court. Curtis also said that Taney's mistaken opinion was not binding on anyone.

RESULTS

Chief Justice Taney had hoped, by ruling on the slavery issue, to put an end to the sectional bickering. Quite the opposite occurred, however. A wave of anger and betrayal swept across the North and Midwest. People who had believed that the Mexican War (1846–1848) was simply a plot by proslavery forces to extend that vile institution now pointed out that this was indeed the case; they said that slave owners could now take their slaves anywhere they wished without penalty. They believed the Supreme Court decision was an assault on free labor and liberty. The South's control of the federal government continued with this decision, said many people in the North. The young Republican Party received thousands of new members because of the *Dred Scott* decision.

Slavery in the Territories? Southerners were overjoyed with this decision. They could now take their property into the new territories without worrying about losing their slaves. The more militant slave owners now demanded that Congress open up all territories to slavery.

By deciding to rule on such a momentous issue, Taney helped widen the already growing rift between North and South. In one stroke, Taney had invalidated the idea of popular sovereignty that had been established by the Kansas-Nebraska Act of 1854, declared the provisions of the Missouri Compromise to be unconstitutional, and smashed the Republican Party's belief that any territory could be closed to slavery.

John Sanford died less than two months after the court decision. Ultimately, Dred Scott was returned to the Blow family, who freed him on May 26, 1857. Scott then worked as a porter, he died in St. Louis in 1858. The Fourteenth Amendment, **ratified** in 1868, gave citizenship to all African Americans.

See also: Kansas-Nebraska Act; Mexican-American War; Popular Sovereignty.

FURTHER READING

Cromwell, Sharon. *Dred Scott v. Sandford: A Slave's Case for Freedom and Citizenship*. Mankato, Minn.: Compass Point Books, 2009.

Finkelman, Paul. *Dred Scott v. Sandford: A Brief History with Documents*. New York: Bedford/St.Martin's, 1997.

McNeese, Timothy. *Dred Scott v. Sandford*. New York: Chelsea House, 2006.

F–G

Filibustering Expeditions

Military excursions against other nations led by American adventurers without the official support of the U.S. government. In general, filibustering expeditions were carried out during the nineteenth century against weak countries of the Caribbean region and Central and South America.

Filibustering excursions were an outgrowth of the belief in Manifest Destiny and were especially supported by farmers in the West and large plantation owners in the South. In many instances, the underlying purpose of the armed incursions was to spread the institution of slavery. Almost all such military ventures were unsuccessful. Because the expedition leaders were usually caught by the nation or **colony** they were invading, they were a source of embarrassment to the U.S. government.

The United States had viewed the island of Cuba as a possible acquisition since at least the time of President Thomas Jefferson (1801–1809). At least 70 filibustering expeditions against Cuba were organized in the United States during the 1800s, none of them successful. In 1810, however, a group of armed American citizens seized West Florida from Spain, which was too weak to fend off the attack. The Republic of Texas and northern Mexico were frequently objects of filibustering activity, but none of these excursions were successful.

Two of the most well-known adventurers who carried out filibustering expeditions were William Walker and Narciso López. Walker, a former American soldier, carried out unsuccessful filibustering expeditions against Baja California; Mexico (1853–1854); Nicaragua (1855–1857); and Honduras (1860). López, a Spanish-American soldier who was supported by prominent slave-holding southerners, attempted to invade Spanish-ruled Cuba in the early 1850s. Both Walker and López were defeated and executed, Walker in Honduras and López in Cuba.

See also: Cuba, Florida.

Florida

Spanish territory in North America acquired by the United States from 1795 through 1819. The acquisition of Florida secured the southern boundary of the United States and allowed the U.S. military to pursue Native Americans who fled to the area after attacking white settlers to the north.

EARLY HISTORY

Spanish explorer Ponce de Leon had traveled around the Florida **peninsula** in 1513. St. Augustine, the oldest permanent European town in North America, was established in 1565 and remained the capital of Spanish Florida until 1821. As a result of the Treaty of Paris of 1763, which ended the French and Indian War (1754–1763), Spain lost Florida to Great Britain, but then regained it from the 1783 Treaty of Paris, which recognized the independence of the United States. Spain, though a monarchy, had sided with the rebels against Great Britain and regained Florida.

BORDER PROBLEMS

Spain also owned the vast Louisiana territory, a huge stretch of land west of the Mississippi River, until France took it over in 1800 then sold it to the United States in 1803. The sale doubled the size of the United States, but the exact borders of the purchase were in doubt, especially when it came to the lower Mississippi River area.

New Boundary Disagreements Arguments over the border erupted quickly after the Louisiana Purchase. President Thomas Jefferson (1801–1809) claimed that West Florida was part of the Louisiana Purchase, but British, French, and Spanish officials told him otherwise. To remedy the situation, Congress in 1804 passed what is called the Mobile Act, the main purpose of which was to extend American **revenue** laws to the Louisiana territory. This bill also claimed American control of all rivers flowing south into the Gulf of Mexico and authorized the president to take control of the town of Mobile (in present-day Alabama) "whenever he shall deem it expedient."

U.S. MOVEMENT INTO
WEST FLORIDA

In September 1810, an American filibustering expedition, or unauthorized military excursion, took control of Baton Rouge, issued a declaration of independence, and asked the United States to **annex** the region. President James Madison (1809–1817) hesitated at first; then, on October 27, he issued a proclamation annexing West Florida as far east as the Pearl River. This area became part of the state of Louisiana in 1812.

U.S. Attempts to Gain Florida In January 1811, Congress passed a "no transfer" resolution. If Spain made an attempt to transfer Florida to any other European power, or if any other country threatened to seize Florida, the United States would take control of Florida because of national preservation. President James Monroe (1817–1825) allowed a filibustering expedition, or unauthorized military undertaking, to move into Florida in March 1812. When it was defeated, however, he claimed no knowledge of its actions.

U.S. Troops Move Into Florida In the summer of 1813, the Creek tribe attacked U.S. settlements in the Mississippi Territory. General Andrew Jackson was placed in command of American forces and decisively defeated the Creek in a series of battles, the last at Horseshoe Bend on March 27, 1814. Jackson pursued the Creek into Florida and temporarily occupied Pensacola while driving the Creek eastward.

END OF SPANISH RULE

Spain's minister to the United States, Don Luis de Onís y Gonzalez, was given instructions to settle the differences between the two nations. Onís and John Quincy Adams, secretary of state under President James Monroe, began serious discussion in early

1818. Onís protested General Jackson's invasion, which he expected would be disavowed by President Monroe. Adams convinced the administration to back the general so that he would have leverage (military action) during the ongoing negotiations with Onís.

The Adams-Onís Treaty Adams and Onís signed the Transcontinental Treaty on February 22, 1819. Better known as the Adams-Onís Treaty, it called for Spain to **cede** Florida to the United States in return for the United States giving up all claims to Texas, which some Americans claimed had been part of the Louisiana Purchase. The United States assumed $5 million in claims by its citizens against Spain for damages caused by Native American raids. The treaty also established a definite border between the United States and Spanish Mexico west of the Mississippi, all the way to the Pacific Ocean.

The Senate quickly voted unanimously to **ratify** the treaty. Spain hesitated because the king was angry over losing Florida. Only after rebellion in 1820 against King Fernando VII (1813–1833) forced him to accept a more limited monarchy was the treaty accepted in Spain. Florida passed into American hands during the summer of 1821. Florida did not become a state until 1845, after costly wars against the Seminole finally allowed the territory's population to grow enough for statehood. Many Seminole were forcibly removed to Indian Territory west of the Mississippi River, in present-day Oklahoma.

See also: Louisiana Purchase; Native Americans; Seminole War; Slavery.

FURTHER READING

Cannavale, Matthew C. *Voices from Colonial America: Florida 1513–1821*. Washington, D.C.: National Geographic Children's Books, 2006.

Gannon, Michael. *Florida: A Short History*. Gainesville: University Press of Florida, 2003.

Gadsden Purchase

American purchase of territory from Mexico in 1854 to define the southern boundary of the United States and allow the construction of a **transcontinental railroad**. This acquisition of territory completed the present-day boundaries of the continental United States.

The Treaty of Guadalupe-Hidalgo, which ended the Mexican-American War (1846–1848), specified that a joint commission from both countries would survey a final boundary between the United States and Mexico. A dispute arose because the town of El Paso was misrepresented on an old map used by the treaty negotiators. The actual site of El Paso favored the Mexican border claim, while the United States waited to see the results of the forthcoming border survey.

The disputed territory included the Mesilla Valley, which bordered the Rio Grande and was composed of flat desert land that was essential for the construction of a railroad. Southern politicians wanted this valley as a means to stake their claim to a southern route for a proposed transcontinental railroad, which would then

United States Expansion, 1783–1854

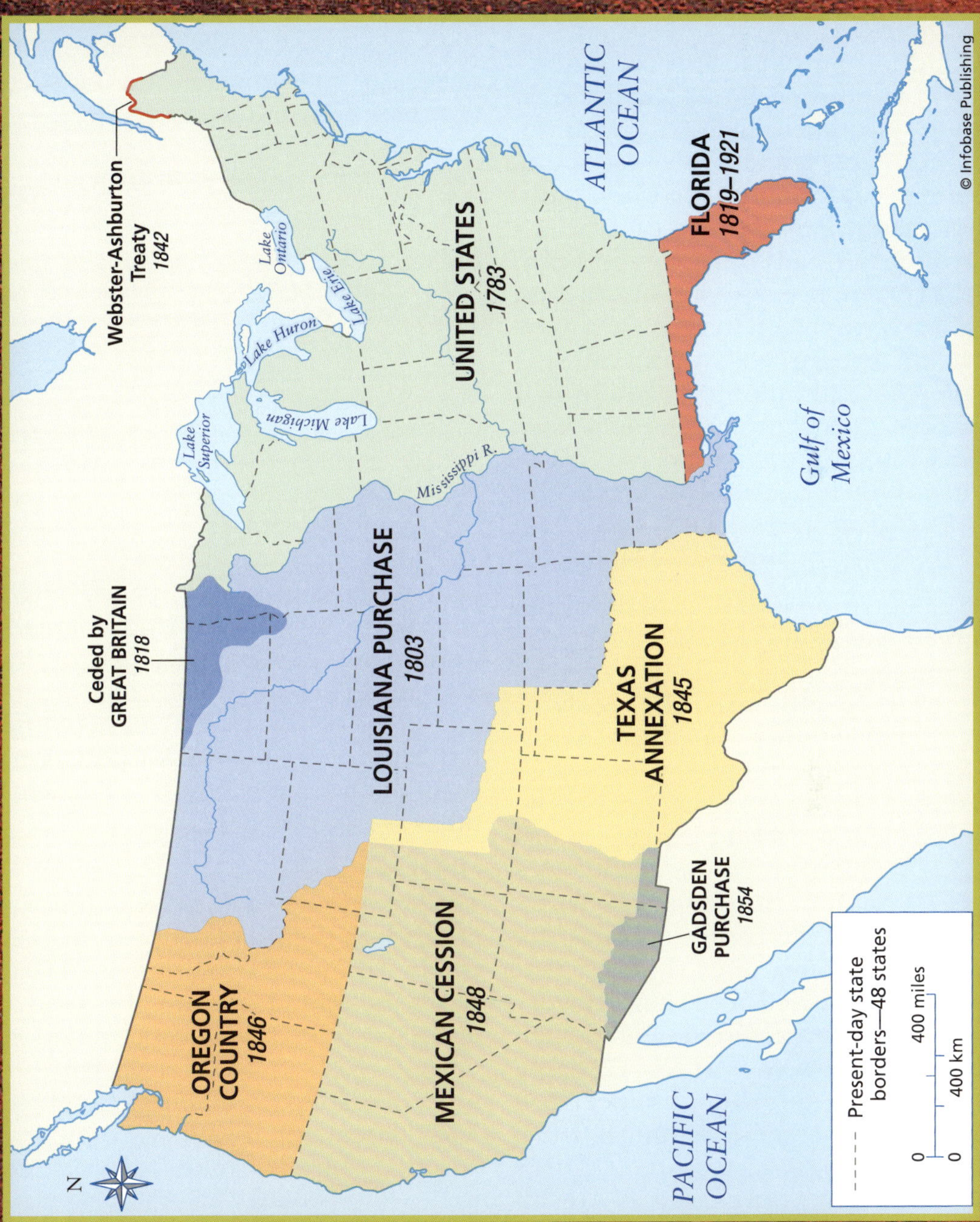

After the United States gained independence in 1783, its western border stretched to the Mississippi River. Within approximately 70 years, the nation expanded across North America to the Pacific Ocean.

link California to the South rather than the North.

DISPUTED LAND

President Franklin Pierce (1853–1857) appointed James Gadsden of South Carolina to negotiate with the Mexican government over the acquisition of the disputed territory. Gadsden was the president of a South Carolina railroad company and a firm believer in the spread of slavery. Gadsden was given instructions to insist on the purchase of the Mesilla Valley for $15 million. In addition, if Mexican president Santa Anna agreed, the United States would pay up to $50 million for parts of several northern Mexican states.

NEGOTIATIONS

After much negotiating, Santa Anna agreed to sell the Mesilla Valley for $15 million. After some delay, President Pierce submitted the treaty to the Senate, which fell three votes short of passing it. Instead, the Senate reduced the amount of land to be purchased by 9,000 square miles (23,309 sq km) and reduced the price to $10 million. Antislavery senators were behind the push to reduce the territory because they worried that the South wished to extend slavery westward. After the Senate passed this treaty by a vote of 33–12, Santa Anna accepted the changes and signed the document on June 8, 1854.

The 26,670 square miles (69,074 sq km) purchased as a result of this treaty included the southern portion of present-day Arizona south of the Gila River and the southwestern corner of present-day New Mexico. Because of the growing division between North and South over slavery, the building of a transcontinental railroad was delayed until after the Civil War (1861–1865). A railroad finally was built through the Gadsden Purchase only in the early 1880s.

See also: Mexican-American War.

FURTHER READING

Devine, David. *Slavery, Scandal, and Steel Rails: The 1854 Gadsden Purchase and the Building of the Second Transcontinental Railroad Across Arizona and New Mexico Twenty-five Years Later*. Bloomington, Ind.: iUniverse, 2004.

Stein, Mark. *How the States Got Their Shapes*. New York: Harper Paperbacks, 2009.

Guam

Pacific island captured by the United States in 1898 during the Spanish-American War. Guam is a part of the Mariana Islands in the Pacific Ocean, 1,500 miles (2,414 km) east of the Philippines, 1,300 miles (2,092 km) from Japan, and 3,000 (4,828 km) miles west of Hawaii.

HISTORY

The Spanish navigator Ferdinand Magellan was the first European to visit Guam, landing there briefly in 1521, when he sailed around the world. Spaniards called the local population "Chamorros," after a local word meaning nobles. Spain claimed Guam in 1565, after which galleons regularly stopped there en route from Mexico to the Philippines.

Although Guam never became an important part of the Spanish Empire, once war broke out between Spain and the United States in April 1898, the island was suddenly noticed by the U.S. After Commodore George Dewey's naval victory in Manila Bay, in the Philippines, U.S. soldiers were sent from San Francisco aboard ships to help capture the Philippines. Captain Henry Glass, commanding the cruiser USS *Charleston*, escorted three troop transports steaming from California to the Philippines. After taking on fresh coal in Honolulu, Hawaii, the captain opened sealed orders that instructed him to stop at Guam and take control of the island.

Early on June 20, 1898, *Charleston* steamed into the harbor at Agana, Guam, and fired several shells at the Spanish fort that protected the harbor. Colonel Juan Marina, the Spanish governor, sent a boat with two officers and Francisco Portusach, a Spanish-born American citizen living on Guam, to greet the American warship.

Captain Glass took the three visitors aboard ship. They informed him that they were sorry that they could not return his salute. They explained that no Spanish supply ship had visited the island since April 9. Because ammunition for their artillery pieces in the fort was in short supply, they could not return the American salute to the Spanish flag.

PEACEFUL SURRENDER

Captain Glass proceeded to inform the surprised Spaniards that their countries were at war. He kept them aboard ship until the next morning, by which time Governor Marina had been informed that a state of war existed. He surrendered the island peacefully. Glass placed the entire Spanish garrison of 60 men aboard one of his ships, leaving Portusach to watch the island. Guam was awarded to the United States in the treaty ending the war.

When the United States officially took control of Guam, President William McKinley (1897–1901) ordered the U.S. Navy to administer the island. While a few naval governors tried to help the Chamorros advance their political standing, most governors ran the island with an iron fist. On December 10, 1941, three days after the Japanese attacked Pearl Harbor, Hawaii, Japanese troops landed on Guam and captured the island. American troops recaptured the island in July-August 1944. The Chamorro people remained loyal to the United States and suffered much during the Japanese occupation.

In 1950, President Harry S. Truman (1945–1953) transferred control of Guam to the Department of the Interior. Guamians are American citizens, but, as residents of an unincorporated territory, they cannot vote for president or elect members of Congress. Guam's acquisition proved important, as the island sits in a strategic location in the Pacific.

See also: McKinley, William; Spanish-American War.

FURTHER READING

Cunningham, Lawrence J., and Janice J. Beaty. *A History of Guam*. Honolulu, Hawaii: Bess Press, 2001.

The Official Portal for the Island of Guam. Available online. URL: http://www.guam.gov.

Taberosi, Danko, and David T. Vann. *Student Atlas of Guam*. Honolulu, Hawaii: Bess Press, 2007.

H–L

Hawaii

Group of Pacific islands that came under U.S. control in a slow process that lasted throughout much of the nineteenth century. The **annexation** of the islands was an essential step as the nation expanded its control throughout the Pacific region.

HISTORY

Hawaii had been explored by British captain James Cook in 1778. The brief contact between Europeans and native Hawaiians brought diseases to the islands that swept through the population, killing hundreds of thousands of people. European contacts grew slowly as merchant vessels of various nations called at Hawaiian ports.

Early Contact Captain Robert Gray was the first American to visit Hawaii (then known as the Sandwich Islands), briefly stopping there in 1789. Beginning in 1820, New England missionaries from the Congregational and Presbyterian churches arrived in Hawaii to bring Christianity to the natives. These strict Christians were horrified at the **animist** religious views of the Hawaiians, along with the public nudity and **polygamy** that were common practice on the islands at the time.

Descendants of these early missionaries took more interest in the potential for economic growth of Hawaii, especially in sugar, which the Hawaiians grew but did not refine. White Americans slowly assumed more and more power in Hawaii, especially during the reign of King Kamehameha III (1825–1854). These *haoles* (Hawaiian for "white foreigners") convinced the king to proclaim a land reform in the late 1840s to facilitate their plan for acquiring land to form plantations. Native Hawaiians had little concept of private land ownership. The Great Mahele land reform allowed foreigners to buy land and dispossess thousands of natives from their property.

Growth of Large Plantations Haoles formed great plantations to raise sugar. Then, when these owners realized that the native Hawaiians did not make good workers, they imported thousands of Chinese and Japanese laborers. The plantations produced large amounts of sugar, but the planters soon discovered that the United States had a protective **tariff** to encourage domestic sugar growers and prevent foreign competition. The *haoles* sought annexation to the United States as a way to solve this problem. In the mid-1850s, because of British protest, President Franklin Pierce (1853–1857) withdrew a treaty that proposed to annex the islands.

CLOSER CONTACT

By the mid-1860s, the United States controlled four-fifths of Hawaii's trade and owned most of the plantations, merchant ships, and whaling vessels. The king's American advisers managed to negotiate a **reciprocity treaty** with the United States in 1867, allowing free trade between Hawaii and the United States. Although a sizable number of congressmen were opposed to free trade, the **expansionists**, who were interested in acquiring more overseas markets, prevailed at this time.

King David Kalakaua (1874–1891) went to Washington, D.C., in 1875 to plead for continuation of reciprocity. The Senate, with President Ulysses S. Grant's (1869–1877) enthusiastic approval, approved the treaty, which turned Hawaii into an American **protectorate**. This treaty gave the United States exclusive rights in Hawaii. The result was a massive growth in Hawaii's sugar production, from 21 million pounds **exported** to America in 1876, to 225 million pounds in 1890.

When the 1875 treaty expired, Louisiana sugar growers tried to block its renewal. King Kalakaua, under instructions from his advisers, offered the United States the exclusive use of Pearl Harbor, and the treaty passed in 1887. The wealthy planters in Hawaii continually looked out for their own power, however. Worried about the king's loyalty to their interests, they forced King Kalakaua to approve a new constitution (the "bayonet constitution") in early 1887. The king was reduced to a figurehead as his cabinet was directly

HISTORY MAKERS

Queen Liliuokalani (1838–1917)

The last reigning monarch of Hawaii, Liliuokalani was 52 years old when she assumed the role of Hawaii's queen in 1891. As the sister of King David Kalakaua, Liliuokalani attended the Golden Jubilee of Queen Victoria in London in 1887.

Liliuokalani inherited Hawaii's throne after her brother's death in January 1891. She was overthrown on January 17, 1893. Although she had the support of her people, the queen decided to avoid bloodshed by allowing herself to be deposed.

Although the United States refused to annex Hawaii and investigated the queen's ouster, the Cleveland administration also did not send troops to restore the queen to her throne, fearing that the use of U.S. troops to oust the Americans responsible for the queen's overthrow would cause an uproar in the United States.

The Republic of Hawaii's new government arrested the queen in January 1895 because her supporters had staged a failed attempt to restore her throne. After a year of imprisonment in the Iolani Palace, during which time Liliuokalani wrote her memoirs and several songs, she was granted a pardon and had her civil rights restored. The former queen lived in Hawaii until her death in 1917. The queen's will gave her estate to be used for orphaned and destitute Hawaiian children. Today, the Queen Liliuokalani Children's Center continues her legacy.

responsible to the local legislature. The constitution also created property qualifications for voting, which meant that most natives were unable to vote. An election later in 1887 solidified the control of the legislature that the wealthy plantation owners already had.

END OF THE KINGDOM OF HAWAII

After King Kalakaua died in 1891, his sister Liliuokalani (1891–1893) became queen. The new monarch was a stronger personality than her late brother, and she made some attempts to exert more control over her kingdom. By the time she came to the throne, Hawaii was experiencing tough economic times. The U.S. Congress had passed the McKinley Tariff of 1890, which allowed sugar from all over the world to enter the United States without taxes, while also compensating domestic growers. Hawaii's sugar crop suffered.

Annexation Plans On January 14, 1893, the queen announced to her advisers that she would be willing to enact a new constitution that curbed the power of the elite *haoles*. Worried members of the Annexation Club, a group that worked behind the scenes to have the United States annex the islands, learned of the queen's plan and hurriedly called a meeting to determine what to do. That night, two of the club members called upon John L. Stevens, the American minister to Hawaii, a man sympathetic to annexation. They asked for American protection and Stevens gave it. Offshore, in the waters of Pearl Harbor, lay the American cruiser USS *Boston*, with a group of United States Marines aboard. Stevens had just returned from a 10-day cruise aboard this warship.

TAKEOVER OF THE ISLANDS

Late in the afternoon of January 16, a force of 162 Marines and sailors landed in Honolulu. On January 17, Queen Liliuokalani was peacefully deposed by the conspirators. Her loyal supporters backed down because of the presence of U.S. troops. A new Republic of Hawaii was proclaimed, with Sanford Dole as its first president.

FINAL ACQUISITION

After some of the Annexation Club members went to Washington, D.C., with the news, President Benjamin Harrison (1889–1893) agreed to an annexation treaty. An emissary from the queen also arrived with his version of the queen's overthrow. The treaty was shelved, however, as Congress adjourned. The new president, Democrat Grover Cleveland (1885–1889, 1893–1897), who was reelected in 1892, frowned on annexation, and the issue was dropped. In 1896, Republican William McKinley won the presidency. He favored annexation, but the treaty failed to get enough Senate votes to pass. More than 90 percent of Hawaiians were opposed to annexation. However, after the Spanish-American War started in 1898, the mood in the United States changed, and the Senate approved annexation of Hawaii on July 6, 1898. The official transfer took place on August 6. Hawaii remained an American territory until 1959, when it became the 50th state.

See also: Guam; Spanish-American War (1898); States, Admission of New.

Further Reading

Kinzer, Stephen. *Overthrow: America's Century of Regime Change from Hawaii to Iraq*. New York: Henry Holt & Company, 2006.

Stone, Scott C. S. *Yesterday in Hawaii: A Voyage Through Time*. Waipahu, Hawaii: Island Heritage Press, 2003.

Kansas-Nebraska Act

In 1854, congressional legislation that established two new territories and allowed residents to determine whether or not slavery could exist in each territory. This act negated the Compromise of 1820, also known as the Missouri Compromise, which prohibited slavery north of Missouri's southern border. By passing this act, Congress fueled the raging slavery debate that now spilled over into the territories as the United States expanded.

POPULAR SOVEREIGNTY

Illinois senator Stephen A. Douglas was the architect of this legislation. Although a Northerner, Douglas believed that compromises had to be made to keep the nation from splitting because of the slavery issue. The senator knew that slavery and its relation to the country's westward expansion was the most explosive political issue of the day.

Douglas believed that the people of each territory should decide the slavery issue for themselves. His theory was called "popular sovereignty" and appealed to Americans who believed in democracy. According to Douglas, each territorial legislature, which was popularly elected by free white males, would decide for each territory on whether or not to allow slavery. Thus, reasoned Douglas, Congress would avoid the sectional interests associated with slavery by deferring to each territory rather than debating the issue in Congress.

PROPOSING THE BILL

Douglas put his popular sovereignty theory to the test in 1854 when the Senate began to consider creating new territories as settlers moved west beyond Missouri. The Compromise of 1820 prohibited slavery north of Missouri's southern border, but Douglas was willing to repeal this compromise because he believed his idea was not only better but would keep the slavery debate out of Congress. Douglas was chair of the Committee on Territories and used his political influence during the heated debate on the bill to create the new territories of Kansas and Nebraska.

Passage of the Act The Senate passed the Kansas-Nebraska Act on May 30, 1854. The bill repealed the Compromise of 1820 and allowed all territories to decide for themselves whether or not to allow slavery. President Franklin Pierce (1853–1857) at first refused to sign the bill because he opposed the repeal of the Compromise of 1820, stating that the compromise had kept the peace for more than 30 years. However, a number of Southern senators informed the president that he would lose their support if he did not sign the new bill, which he finally did.

A National Figure Senator Douglas received national attention for his role in the Kansas-Nebraska Act. However, the kind of attention he received was not what he wanted, and it hurt his future run for president in 1860. Northerners accused Douglas of abandoning his morality in his desire to run for president. They felt he had given in to the proslavery argument in an effort to build a broad base for his political goals. Douglas's advocacy of popular sovereignty helped create the Republican Party, which was against expansion of slavery in the territories. In 1858, when Douglas was up for reelection in Illinois, he debated a relatively unknown politician named Abraham Lincoln, who ran against him as the Republican candidate. Although Lincoln did not win the Senate seat, he earned national recognition for his debate with Douglas over slavery in the territories.

In the South, Democrats assailed Douglas because most Southerners recognized the fact that slavery would not likely flourish throughout most of the region. A possible exception however, was the area of eastern Kansas. The colder, shorter growing season of the Great Plains meant that cotton and other labor-intensive crops that involved slaves would not work well there. Many people accused Douglas of pandering to both sections of the country in an effort to ensure that any transcontinental railroad that ran through the new territories would be based out of Chicago in Douglas's home state.

Trouble in Kansas Once the bill passed, both proslavery and antislavery forces in Kansas tried to sway voters. The Kansas Territory erupted into civil war, resulting in more than 200 deaths and much property destruction. Governor after governor was unable to control the escalating violence. At one time, there were two competing territorial legislatures, one proslavery, one antislavery. Presidents Pierce and James Buchanan (1857–1861) did little to end the violence. Congress did not have luck either. Kansas was finally admitted to the Union as the 35th state in 1861 with an antislavery constitution.

ELECTION OF 1860

Senator Douglas ran for president in 1860. However, because of the divisiveness of the slavery issue, the Democratic Party splintered into sectional **factions** with two candidates—Douglas representing the North and John C. Breckinridge representing the South. A third party, the Constitutional Union Party, also emerged. Republican Abraham Lincoln won the election with only 40 percent of the popular vote.

See also: Douglas, Stephen A.; Slavery.

FURTHER READING

Johannsen, Robert. *The Frontier, the Union, and Stephen A. Douglas*. Urbana: University of Illinois Press, 1989.

McArthur, Debra. *The Kansas-Nebraska Act and Bleeding Kansas in American History*. Berkeley Heights, N.J.: Enslow Publishers, 2003.

Lewis and Clark Expedition

From 1803 to 1806, exploration by members of a U.S. scouting party of the northern area of the Louisiana Purchase, Rocky Mountains, and Pacific coast. This was the first American expedition across the North American continent and has become the subject of one of the most popular stories of American history. The findings of the expedition laid the foundation for further expansion of the United States.

ORIGINS OF THE EXPEDITION

President Thomas Jefferson (1801–1809) supervised the purchase of the Louisiana Territory from France in early 1803. The president had wanted to acquire only the New Orleans area to ensure a smooth flow of commerce down the Mississippi River.

Guided by Sacajawea, explorers Meriwether Lewis and William Clark, leaders of the Corps of Discovery, reached the mouth of the Columbia River, where it enters the Pacific Ocean, in November 1805. After securing the purchase of the vast Louisiana Territory, President Thomas Jefferson sent the expedition westward to find out as much as possible about the inhabitants of this new land.

Napoleon, the ruler of France, owing to the difficulties France faced in Europe, decided to sell Louisiana in its entirety. The United States paid $15 million for 827,000 square miles (214,192,016 hectares).

Even before the Louisiana Purchase was finalized, Jefferson asked Congress for $2,500 to fund an expedition to explore the West. Jefferson realized that the nation did not have a good sense of the geography west of the Mississippi, especially of the Missouri River, one of the Mississippi's chief **tributaries** that flowed into the Mississippi at St. Louis. Therefore, he reasoned, it would make good sense to send a small group of men to investigate both the geography of the West and its Native American inhabitants.

Selecting the Crew Jefferson selected his personal secretary, Captain Meriwether Lewis, to lead the expedition. Lewis in turn called upon William Clark as a partner to help lead the Corps of Discovery, as it became known. Clark was the younger brother of Revolutionary War hero George Rogers Clark, who had retired from army service in 1796 as a second lieutenant. Lewis had a keelboat constructed in Pittsburgh, then floated down the Ohio River, picking up men and supplies as he went. As finally assembled near St. Louis, the expedition included 33 men, as well as Lewis's dog, Seaman.

Goals of Exploration On June 20, 1803, Jefferson penned a letter to Captain Lewis. "The object of your mission," wrote the president, "is to explore the Missouri River, and such

principal stream of it, as by its course and communication with the water of the Pacific Ocean, whether the Columbia, Oregan [sic], Colorado or any other river may offer the most direct and practicable water communication across this continent, for the purposes of commerce." Lewis was also directed to examine the possibilities for fur trading and to learn all he could about the Native American tribes, animals, and plants seen during the expedition.

1804: HEADING UP THE MISSOURI RIVER

Lewis and Clark left the St. Louis area on May 14, 1804, after spending the winter getting ready. The men steered the keelboat up the wide Missouri River. In early August, they met two local Native American tribes, giving them gifts of peace before heading upriver. The expedition's only fatality took place on August 20, when Charles Floyd died, probably from a burst appendix.

By the end of October, the expedition had reached the vicinity of present-day Bismarck, North Dakota, where they met the friendly Mandan and Hidatsa tribes. Lewis and Clark decided to stop before winter set in, so they erected a small fort near the native village and settled in for the winter. While spending the time at this location, Lewis hired a French-Canadian fur trapper named Toussaint Charbonneau as an interpreter. His wife was Sacajawea, a member of the Shoshone tribe. She had been captured and sold to Charbonneau. Lewis and Clark decided to take her along with them in 1805, after she in-

HISTORY MAKERS
Sacajawea (c. 1790–1812)

Ever since her association with the Lewis and Clark expedition, Sacajawea has become an American icon. Very little is actually known about this courageous Shoshone woman. She seems to have been born some time around 1790, the daughter of a Shoshone chief. Sacajawea was kidnapped by the Hidatsa tribe during a raid and sold to French-Canadian fur trapper Toussaint Charbonneau.

When the Lewis and Clark expedition reached the Mandan tribe on the upper Missouri River and wintered there in 1804–1805, the explorers hired Charbonneau to go with them as an interpreter. Sacajawea also went along, for Clark noted that "a woman with a party of men is a token of peace." Two months before the expedition left the Mandan, Sacajawea gave birth to a son whom she named Jean Baptiste. Clark called him Pomp or Pompey.

When the expedition reached Shoshone territory, Sacajawea was overjoyed to find that her brother was now chief. Instead of remaining behind, she helped the expedition secure horses for the trip through the Rockies. Sacajawea, her husband, and her child all completed the trek to the Pacific Ocean. On the expedition's return, the Charbonneau family returned to the Hidatsa tribe.

In 1809, Charbonneau went to St. Louis with his son. When he left to return to fur trapping, Charbonneau left Pomp with Clark. Sources disagree about whether or not Sacajawea came to St. Louis with her husband. A few sources indicate that she did, and then returned to her home, where she died of fever in 1812. Native American oral traditions state that she returned to her own people, the Shoshone, and lived until 1884. Sacajawea was used as a symbol of a strong and independent woman by early advocates of women's **suffrage**. In 2000, the United States released a dollar coin with Sacajawea's image on the obverse, or front.

---

formed them that her tribe lived near the sources of the Missouri River.

1805: TO THE PACIFIC OCEAN

On April 7, 1805, Lewis and Clark sent the keelboat and a dozen men back down the Missouri with maps, reports, and artifacts collected during their voyage upriver. The rest of the expedition headed west via canoe. The party encountered a grizzly bear on April 29 and had difficulty slaying it; no one had ever seen one before. This took place near where the Yellowstone River entered the Missouri.

On June 2, the party arrived at a fork in the river that did not appear on the faulty maps they possessed. After some investigation up both rivers, they took the southern fork, which proved to be the Missouri. By mid-June, they had proceeded far enough to discover the Great Falls of the Missouri, a series of four waterfalls that made it impossible for the men to continue with their canoes. The men had to **portage** their equipment for 18 miles (29 km) before continuing the journey. By late July, the expedition reached the three forks of the Missouri, which they named for Secretary of the Treasury Albert Gallatin, Secretary of State James Madison, and President Jefferson.

Moving Westward The party headed southwest along the Jefferson River, where, on August 12, Captain Lewis climbed a ridge and reached the **Continental Divide**. He quickly came to the conclusion that there was no easy passage through the Rocky Mountains, as was previously thought. Sacajawea began to recognize landmarks and guided the expedition to a major Shoshone camp, where she found her brother was now chief. On the last day of August, the expedition again set off west through the mountains, using 29 horses and a mule.

Almost a month later, the expedition emerged from the Rockies starving, having exhausted their supplies during the 160-mile (257-km) crossing of the Bitterroot Range. Near present-day Weippe, Idaho, the men encountered a village of the Nez Perce tribe. This tribe proved to be friendly. They showed the Americans how to build excellent dugout canoes, which the party used to continue their journey down the Clearwater and Snake rivers, reach-ing the Columbia River on October 16, 1805.

On to the Pacific Ocean The expedition continued down the Columbia, meeting several local tribes en route. The trip involved two portages around the Dalles rapids and Celilo falls. On October 30, the men had one last portage around the 10-mile (16-km) stretch of the Columbia known as the Cascades. Once they passed this area on November 7, Clark wrote in his journal that he thought he could see the Pacific Ocean. In reality, they had only arrived at the spot where the Columbia grew very wide before reaching the ocean. Severe storms then drenched the region, forcing a halt for nearly three weeks. Finally, the expedition gazed upon the Pacific Ocean. On November 24, the expedition voted to cross to the south side of the Columbia and erect winter quarters, which they named Fort Clatsop after a local tribe.

1806: RETURN TO THE UNITED STATES

The Lewis and Clark expedition wintered at Fort Clatsop until March 23, 1806, when the men presented the log structure to the local tribe and headed up the Columbia River toward home. After passing the rapids, the men abandoned their dugout canoes and proceeded on foot until they reached the base of the Bitterroot Mountains, where they had to stop and wait for more than a month for the snow to melt enough to proceed. The expedition stayed with the Nez Perce during this time. Captain Lewis described them as "the most hospitable, honest and sincere people that we have met with in our voyage."

After crossing the Bitterroots, Lewis and Clark divided the expedition into smaller groups in order to explore more territory. The parties reunited at the mouth of the Yellowstone River on August 12. Two days later, the men arrived at the Mandan village where they had stayed back in 1804. Here, Sacajawea and her husband remained, along with one of the Americans, who was given permission to return to the Yellowstone to trap beaver.

Lewis and Clark's men moved fast with the current down the Missouri River and reached St. Louis on September 23, 1806. Once word was sent back east, the men became national heroes. Lewis was named governor of the Louisiana Territory, and Clark became Indian agent for the West. The expedition's official report was published in 1814. During the trip, Lewis and Clark drew about 140 maps, the first accurate mapping of the territory through which they had traveled. Word of the abundant animals in the mountains led to the evolution of **"mountain men"** who went out west to trap beaver and sell their furs. These men added to the geographical knowledge amassed by Lewis and Clark and helped spread U.S. interest in the West.

See also: Louisiana Purchase.

FURTHER READING

Ambrose, Stephen E. *Undaunted Courage: Meriwether Lewis, Thomas Jefferson, and the Opening of the American West*. New York: Simon & Schuster, 1996.

Ditchfield, Christin. *The Lewis and Clark Expedition*. Danbury, Conn.: Children's Press, 2006.

Isserman, Maurice. *Across America: The Lewis and Clark Expedition*. New York: Facts On File, 2004.

Lincoln, Abraham (1809–1865)

Sixteenth president (1861–1865) of the United States and considered by many to be the nation's greatest president. Abraham Lincoln saw the country through the Civil War (1861–1865), the nation's most trying and bloodiest episode.

EARLY LIFE

Born on February 12, 1809, in Hodgenville, Kentucky, Lincoln's early life was difficult, hacked out of the wilderness of Indiana, where the family settled when Lincoln was a child. His family lived in a log lean-to while his father built a permanent cabin on farmland on which they were squatting. Young Abraham farmed and cleared land. When he was nine, his mother died, but a year later his father remarried. Lincoln had very little formal schooling, about a year, all told, though he developed an appetite for reading.

In 1830, after spending his youth in Indiana, Lincoln and his family moved to Illinois. At age 21, he left his father's farm. He worked in a variety of careers but wanted to be a politician. At age 23, he ran for a seat in the Illinois General Assembly as a member of the Whig Party. He lost, but he ran again in 1834 and was elected. It was around this time that he began to teach himself law. Within three years, he had learned enough to pass the bar. In 1837, he moved to Springfield to begin his law practice.

Lincoln was an immensely successful lawyer. He gained a reputation for being sharp in cross-examinations, and his closing arguments were renowned for their persuasiveness. Lincoln became the leader of the Whig Party in Illinois and served for many years in the Illinois General Assembly. In 1846, Lincoln was elected to the U.S. House of Representatives, where he served only one term.

PROTESTING WAR

It was during his short time as a representative that Lincoln made his mark on the national stage with his protests against the Mexican War (1846–1848). In fact, Lincoln became the leading voice of the Whig Party against the war.

In 1845, the United States had annexed Texas. However, there was disagreement between Mexico and the United States as to the location of the Texan border. Mexico claimed it was the Nueces River, while the United States claimed it was the Rio Grande, which was farther south. In September 1845, President Polk (1845–1849) sent an envoy to Mexico City to settle the dispute and buy the territories of New Mexico and California. Because the Mexican president refused to even speak to the envoy, in early 1846 President Polk ordered the U.S. Army to take up positions along the Rio Grande, occupying the disputed land. On April 25, 1846, Mexican troops crossed the Rio Grande to fight with U.S. troops.

CLAIMS OF OPPORTUNISM

Lincoln condemned the war. He claimed that the president was pursuing glory more than reasonable goals. He did not believe that the Texas border extended to the Rio Grande. Further, he did not believe the president's claim that war was necessary because American blood had been shed on American soil. Lincoln demanded to know the "spot" on which such blood was shed, which became known as the Spot Resolutions. Despite his condemnation, Lincoln did vote to supply the military during the war.

Lincoln's opposition to the war brought him little favor. Many Whigs thought it was a dangerous position and refused to support the Spot Resolutions. Historians cannot decide how much Lincoln's position against the war cost him politically. Later, in the 1850s, Lincoln emerged as a leader of the new Republican Party and won the presidency in the election of 1860.

See also: Douglas, Stephen A., Mexican-American War.

FURTHER READING

Wheelan, Joseph. *Invading Mexico: America's Continental Dream and the Mexican War, 1846–1848*. New York: PublicAffairs, 2007.

Louisiana Purchase

American acquisition in 1803 of a vast territory west of the Mississippi

River, an area that doubled the size of the United States. At the close of the Revolutionary War (1775–1783), the new United States was surrounded by potential enemies. Canada to the north was part of the British Empire. Florida to the south and Louisiana to the west were part of the Spanish Empire. Although Spain had supported U.S. independence, Spain was still a monarchy, and worried about the effects of a democracy adjacent to its North American possessions.

AMERICAN TRADE CONCERNS

American expansion west of the Appalachian Mountains increased after the Revolutionary War. Kentucky became a state in 1792 and Tennessee in 1796. The Northwest Territory was organized in the 1780s as settlers began to move into this area once the Native Americans were defeated and pushed aside. Other settlers began to enter the future states of Mississippi and Alabama.

American settlements west of the Appalachians relied on the Mississippi River and its **tributaries** for trade. It was far easier to ship products (such as corn and lumber) down the Mississippi to New Orleans, than over rough roads to Eastern buyers. However, Spanish officials refused to allow American goods to reach New Orleans for several years. The Spanish finally changed their minds when they realized that the growing American population far outnumbered their own in Louisiana. In 1795, the United States negotiated a treaty with Spain that allowed Americans the "right of deposit" in New Orleans–the right to leave goods in New Orleans warehouses to await shipment in sea-going vessels.

FRANCE TAKES CONTROL OF LOUISIANA

In October 1800, Napoleon, the ruler of France, signed a secret treaty with Spain, in which Spain gave Louisiana to France in return for the Spanish king's brother-in-law becoming the ruler of a small Italian kingdom. France kept Spanish officials in their administrative positions in Louisiana. In October 1802, one of these officials, acting under orders from King Carlos IV (1788–1808), revoked the right of Americans to keep their goods in New Orleans. President Thomas Jefferson (1801–1809) was concerned about this development. "There is on the globe," he wrote, "one single spot, the possessor of which is our natural and habitual enemy. It is New Orleans, through which the produce of three-eighths of our territory must pass to market."

Napoleon hoped to use Louisiana to reestablish a French presence in North America. He also hoped to recapture Haiti, a former Caribbean possession of France. France had abolished slavery in 1794, by which time former slaves had taken control of Haiti. Napoleon signed a peace treaty with Great Britain in 1801 and sent an army to capture its former colony. Tropical diseases and ferocious resistance by Haitians, however, destroyed the French army. Napoleon had planned to send troops to Louisiana, but the failure of his expedition to Haiti forced him to cancel plans.

On April 30, 1803, American diplomats in France signed the treaty acquiring the vast Louisiana Territory from France. The purchase expanded the western border of the United States to the Rocky Mountains.

PURCHASE OF LOUISIANA

Spanish king Carlos IV ordered the reopening of the Mississippi in February 1803, and by May, New Orleans was open to U.S. traffic. In the meantime, President Jefferson, in January 1803, sent James Monroe to Paris to work with Ambassador Robert Livingston "to procure a cession of New Orleans and the Floridas to the United States." Congress appropriated $2 million for the purchase.

Monroe arrived in Paris in April 1803. Livingston had previously suggested to the French that they sell Louisiana to the United States, but had gotten nowhere. The day before Monroe reached Paris, the French foreign minister, Tallyrand, caught Livingston off guard by suggesting that France was interested in selling much more than New Orleans. Napoleon by this point had decided that Louisiana was indefensible if he got into a war with the British. He thought it was far better to sell the area, rather than have Great Britain seize it during a war.

Livingston, Monroe, and François Barbé-Marbois signed a treaty on April 30. France sold the entire Louisiana Territory to the United States for $11,250,000. America received 827,000 square miles (214,192,016 hectares) for the money, an average of 3.5 cents per acre.

Jefferson announced the treaty on July 4. Although there was some opposition to the treaty, it passed through the Senate successfully. Jefferson, though, worried that the purchase was unconstitutional, but his advisers convinced him not to seek a constitutional amendment that might take years and perhaps nullify the acquisition of so much land.

FURTHER READING

McNeese, Timothy. *The Louisiana Purchase: Growth of a Nation.* New York: Chelsea House Publications, 2008.

Nelson, Sheila. *Thomas Jefferson's America: The Louisiana Purchase, 1800–1811.* Broomall, Pa.: Mason Crest Publishers, 2005.

M–N

Manifest Destiny

The idea that the United States was destined to spread westward and occupy much of the North American continent. Although the term itself was popularized by John L. O'Sullivan in an 1845 magazine article, the process identified by historians as "manifest destiny" was in place decades before O'Sullivan's article.

BACKGROUND

In 1783, at the end of the American Revolution (1775–1783), the new United States included 13 former British **colonies** with a population of fewer than 4 million people, most of whom lived east of the Appalachian Mountains. Less than 70 years later, in 1850, the federal **census** of that year counted more than 23 million people stretched from Maine to California. Historians have tried to explain this rapid territorial expansion by using the manifest destiny idea, namely that it was the destiny of the United States to expand from ocean to ocean.

Nationalist Feelings

The concept of manifest destiny also means that Americans needed to have a strong belief in nationalism—the love of, and pride in, one's country. During colonial times and throughout much of American history, many American leaders sincerely believed that the United States was a special nation. They believed God had given the American people the special mission of bringing democracy to the world, to be a model republic that the rest of the world would attempt to copy for itself.

Gaining Land

Manifest destiny often includes the idea of imperialism—the acquisition of land (territory) from other countries or peoples in order to extend the territory and influence of one's own country. Imperialism can be aggressive, as in the case of many European countries, such as Spain, France, and Great Britain during the age of exploration. Thomas Jefferson (1801–1809) once wrote that America had to expand its "empire of Liberty" to bring the ideals of American civilization to other people.

CONTROVERSY

Today, most modern historians argue that the westward expansion of the United States was not inevitable but rather a deliberate process guided by numerous politicians throughout the nineteenth century. Some historians believe that **expansionists** used the idea of manifest destiny to sell their imperialistic plans to the common people.

Opposition to the continued expansion of the United States existed from the early days of the nation. When Jefferson proposed purchasing Louisiana, members of the **Federalist Party** objected, stating that the distance from the national capital to Louisiana was too far for democracy to have any effect. **Abolitionists** objected to the acquisition of Texas because they wanted to keep slavery from spreading into the new territory. President Grover Cleveland (1885–1889, 1893–1897) refused to **annex** Hawaii. He called annexation "a perversion of our national mission. The mission of our nation is to build up and make a greater country out of what we have instead of annexing islands."

IN THE NINETEENTH CENTURY

The highpoint of manifest destiny was the 1840s. Before that time, the United States had expanded at a much slower pace. President Thomas Jefferson had pushed to acquire New Orleans by purchase from France to safeguard American commercial access to the city, thus allowing Western farmers and businesses to ship their goods by sea. Napoleon's 1803 decision to sell the entire Louisiana Territory was an unexpected opportunity for Jefferson to expand the nation's western border and ensure that the Mississippi River and its tributaries would remain in the nation's hands.

Obtaining Florida The United States acquired Florida from Spain in 1819 as part of a treaty that specified the western border between the United States and Spanish Mexico. Florida had been a refuge for escaped slaves as well as hostile Native Americans. American interest in acquiring Florida stemmed from the desire to strengthen and pacify the nation's southern border.

The acquisition of Florida in 1819 was followed by a period during which the United States did not expand much. As settlers moved west across the Mississippi, the issue of whether slavery would be allowed in new territories jumped onto the national stage and did not leave until 1865. The Compromise of 1820 (the Missouri Compromise) tried to settle this issue but only delayed its end. Throughout the 1830s, American settlers moved into Texas, then a province of Mexico. They revolted in 1836 and established an independent republic. Calls for annexation to the United States were unsuccessful because of the slavery issue, which prevented widespread support for annexation.

Further Expansion American pioneers also crossed the Great Plains and Rocky Mountains to settle in the Oregon Territory, beginning in the late 1830s. This territory was disputed between the United States and Great Britain. Other settlers moved into California, another Mexican province. Filibustering expeditions, or unauthorized military excursions, into Texas, as well as into Central America, failed because of the lack of popular American support for such raids.

President James K. Polk (1845–1849) has long been considered the most influential advocate of manifest destiny. Polk was an aggressive **expansionist**. He wanted to settle the Oregon question and also acquire California, which contained the best port (present-day San Francisco) on the entire West Coast. The president pushed the United States into a war with Mexico after annexing Texas and arguing about where the southern boundary of Texas was located. The Mexican-American War (1846–

1848) resulted in the addition of California and the Southwest to the United States. The favorable settlement of the Oregon question with Great Britain, which peacefully established the border between the United States and British Canada at the 49th parallel, meant that the United States jumped from the edge of the Great Plains to the Pacific Ocean in only a few years during the 1840s.

Manifest destiny ignored the fact that American expansion did not take place in uninhabited land. The very idea of manifest destiny implied a superiority of American democracy and civilization. Native Americans were continually swept aside or annihilated as the United States expanded. Many Americans looked down on Spanish civilization and did not treat the Hispanic residents of the region very well as the country expanded and acquired Texas, California, and the Southwest.

FURTHER READING

Joy, Mark S. *American Expansionism, 1783–1860: A Manifest Destiny?* London: Pearson Education Limited, 2003.

Mexican-American War (1846–1848)

War that resulted in American acquisition of almost 40 percent of Mexican territory as a result of the peace treaty ending this conflict. The outcome of the war greatly expanded the borders of the United States and fulfilled the ideal of manifest destiny—that the nation should reach from coast to coast.

ROOTS OF THE WAR

The origins of the conflict stemmed from the 1844 U.S. presidential election, in which James K. Polk (1845–1849), the Democratic candidate, emerged victorious. The Democratic Party platform called for the **annexation** of Texas, recognizing the Rio Grande as the southern boundary of Texas.

Thinking that the election results boded well for Texas annexation, **lame duck** president John Tyler (1841–1845) presented a joint resolution to Congress that provided for the annexation of Texas. It passed unanimously on February 28, 1845, four days before Polk was sworn into office. As a result, Mexico broke diplomatic relations with the United States.

FAILED DIPLOMACY WITH MEXICO

President Polk was an eager **expansionist**. After Texas approved annexation on July 4, 1845, Polk decided to try to negotiate with Mexico to end the diplomatic impasse. He sent Louisiana politician John Slidell to Mexico City in the fall of 1845. Slidell was authorized to pay up to $25 million to Mexico in exchange for their provinces of California and New Mexico; in return, the United States would absorb all monetary claims by American citizens against Mexico since Texas independence in 1836.

Polk's outlook was too simplistic for such diplomacy to succeed. Mexican national pride had been hurt because of Texas independence. The U.S. annexation of Texas further angered Mexico. Mexico was also angry at the Texas claim that its southern boundary was the Rio Grande, when historically the Mexican province of Texas had the Nueces River–120 miles (193 km) farther north–as its boundary. Thus, the Mexican government refused to talk with Slidell. For even allowing Slidell to enter the capital, the Mexican president was overthrown by General Mariano Paredes, a hardliner who wanted nothing to do with the United States.

WAR BEGINS

When it became apparent that Slidell's mission was a failure, Polk, on January 13, 1846, sent orders to General Zachary Taylor to advance his 4,000 soldiers across the Nueces River and build a fort on the north bank of the Rio Grande, near the river's mouth. Polk's action was a bold, confrontational move that he surely knew would anger the Mexicans. They responded by first sending an ultimatum, or final warning, to Taylor, telling him to withdraw. After Taylor's own offer of negotiation was ignored, a large Mexican cavalry force crossed the river and attacked one of Taylor's patrols on April 25. Polk received word of the attack on May 9. Polk then asked Congress to declare war, which it did on May 13, the House voting 174–14 in favor, while the Senate voted 40–2 for war.

GENERAL TAYLOR'S CAMPAIGN

Even before Congress declared war, Taylor's troops had fought two small battles against a larger Mexican army that crossed the river to attack the fort Taylor's men had built. The United States won both engagements–Palo Alto on May 8 and Resaca de la Palma on May 9–driving the enemy across the river and occupying the city of Matamoros. Then, Taylor had to wait for three months while supplies and volunteer soldiers reached his position.

With 6,000 men, Taylor left Matamoros in August, heading for the city of Monterrey, which was defended by a Mexican force of 10,000 men. In three days of hard fighting, Taylor's men suffered more than 500 casualties but captured Monterrey. The general then granted an eight-week **armistice** to allow both governments to decide what to do next. Polk was furious with Taylor and rescinded the armistice. Taylor then advanced south to Satillo, where his army went into winter camp.

Polk then decided to change strategy. His advisers decided that it would be easier to attack Mexico City by landing troops on the coast and marching directly on the city, rather than continuing overland through rough terrain. Polk was also jealous of Taylor's victories. Taylor was a Whig, and Polk thought his rising popularity might lead to a future run for the presidency. Taylor was thus stripped of most of his troops, leaving him with only 5,000 men to defend his gains. General Santa Anna, who had become president of Mexico, organized a new army and marched north to confront Taylor. Santa Anna attacked in the two-day Battle of Buena Vista (February 22–23, 1847), but suffered defeat and retreated. This battle ended the war in northern Mexico.

CALIFORNIA AND NEW MEXICO

One of President Polk's aims was to acquire California for the United

States. He knew that Great Britain was interested in the area, and he wished to keep the region for his own growing country. As soon as war was declared, American troops headed for California. A small force led by Captain John C. Frémont moved south from Oregon and helped establish a temporary republic in northern and central California as Marines and sailors from U.S. warships landed in southern California.

Shortly after war began, Polk ordered Colonel Stephen W. Kearny to seize Santa Fe, the capital of New Mexico province. Kearny and 1,700 men left Fort Leavenworth in late June and took control of Santa Fe on August 18. Leaving a **garrison** in Santa Fe, Kearny then marched westward toward California with about 300 men. He also sent Colonel Alexander W. Doniphan, along with 850 Missouri mounted soldiers, south into Mexico. Doniphan's troops captured the Mexican state of Chihuahua on March 1, 1847, and then continued on to Satillo, the capital city of the Mexican state of Coahuila, where he arrived on May 21, having marched 3,500 miles (5,633 km).

Kearny's men arrived in southern California in early December, just in time to help crush a rebellion against American occupation. By early January 1847, California was in American hands.

GENERAL SCOTT'S CAMPAIGN

After deciding to attack Mexico City directly, Polk ordered General Winfield Scott, the army's senior general, to lead the attack. Scott assembled 10,000 troops, which landed at the port of Veracruz on March 9, 1847.

Scott deployed heavy artillery batteries to bombard the walled city, which surrendered on March 29.

The paved National Road led westward from Veracruz some 200 miles (322 km) to Mexico City. Scott used this road for his advance, quickly leaving the coastal plain to prevent an outbreak of **yellow fever** from devastating his army.

The U.S. troops left Veracruz on April 8. Santa Anna, with yet another reorganized army, blocked the U.S. advance at a point where the National Road passed through several high hills on both sides of the road. His 12,000 men outnumbered Scott's 8,500 troops. As the U.S. troops paused to consider what to do, engineer officers, including Lieutenant Robert E. Lee, found a mountain trail that enabled U.S. soldiers to outflank Santa Anna's position. During the two-day Battle of Cerro Gordo (April 17–18), Scott's troops routed the Mexicans, inflicting more than 4,000 casualties while losing only 417 themselves.

By May 15, Scott's army was at the city of Puebla, 75 miles (121 km) from Mexico City. Scott halted to wait for reinforcements and fresh supplies. He left Puebla on August 7, taking a limited amount of supplies with him so that he would not have to detach men to guard a lengthening supply line.

After scouting the strong defenses of the Mexican capital, Scott circled to the south to attack. Santa Anna had about 30,000 men to defend the city, while Scott moved approximately 8,000 men into position. In the battles of Contreras and Churubusco on August 20, Scott's men suffered heavy casualties—1,052 men killed, wounded, and missing—while the Mexicans lost at least 9,000 soldiers, one-third of their army. Santa Anna retreated behind the city walls to await the next U.S. attack.

However, an armistice went into effect on August 25 to allow peace talks to begin. State Department clerk Nicholas P. Trist had arrived from Washington, D.C., with instructions from President Polk to negotiate a peace treaty. However, the initial negotiations with Santa Anna proved to be futile. Hardliners in the government refused much of the U.S. offer.

Scott canceled the armistice on September 7. The next day, U.S. troops won the Battle of Molino del Rey. On September 13, U.S. troops captured the fortress of Chapultepec, the last Mexican position outside the city. Scott's men assaulted the city walls on September 14, breaking through into the city, which Santa Anna abandoned.

PEACE NEGOTIATIONS

Though U.S. troops captured Mexico City, the government fled to a town 125 miles (201 km) from the capital. Santa Anna, humiliated, resigned as president and was replaced by Manuel de la Peña y Peña, a man willing to negotiate in good faith, even though it might cost him his job.

On the U.S. side, Polk was eager to end the war, which was costing much more money than originally thought. The longer the war went on, the more and more disenchanted the American people were becoming. Even as the war began, many Northerners believed that the conflict was a plot by Southern slaveholders to grab more territory to expand slavery.

A growing number of Democrats were beginning to cry "all of Mexico," hoping to cash in on the army's victory by annexing the entire country of Mexico. Polk was opposed to this and hoped that negotiations would quickly come to an end before his opponents had their way. Many Southerners opposed annexing Mexico because that country had abolished slavery and would never accept it again. Other Americans argued that it would not be good to annex a country filled with nonwhite peoples.

Peace negotiations finally began after the Mexican government appointed a new interim president, who got rid of most of the hardliners and asked Peña y Peña to be the chief peace negotiator. Because of the delay in getting started, coupled with Trist's earlier failure during the August-September truce, Polk decided to replace Trist with another diplomat. By the time Trist received word of his recall to Washington on November 16, he was in the midst of positive negotiations and thus ignored Polk's order.

THE PEACE TREATY

While the Mexicans continued to delay, General Scott advised them that he would annex even more territory as more reinforcements began to arrive and that his men would start collecting taxes to pay for the occupation. Peña y Peña then instructed his peace commission to accept Trist's terms.

Mexican and American commissioners signed the Treaty of Guadalupe Hidalgo on February 2, 1848. Under the terms of this treaty, the U.S.-Mexican boundary was established along the Rio Grande, then west to the Gila River, up that river to its junction with the Colorado River, and then straight west to the Pacific Ocean. Mexican citizens living in the vast territory—about a half million square miles—annexed by the United States could remain and become American citizens or move south to Mexico. Mexico would receive $15 million and the United States would pay debts owed to American citizens by Mexico. Although angered by Trist's disobedience of orders, Polk presented the treaty to the Senate, which **ratified** it on March 10, 1848, by a vote of 38–14. The Mexican Congress approved it on May 19. The war added the future states of California, Nevada, Utah, and parts of Colorado, Arizona, and New Mexico to the United States.

See also: California; Polk, James K.; Texas; Wilmot Proviso.

FURTHER READING

Casey, Charles W. *The Mexican War: Mr. Polk's War*. Berkeley Heights, N.J.: Enslow Publishing, 2002.

Feldman, Ruth T. *The Mexican-American War*. Minneapolis, Minn.: Lerner Publishing, 2004.

Meed, Douglas V. *The Mexican War, 1846–1848*. New York: Routledge, 2003.

Nardo, Don. *The Mexican-American War*. Farmington Hills, Mich.: Greenhaven Press, 1999.

Mormons

See Utah Territory.

Native Americans

The original inhabitants of the Western Hemisphere, first called "Indians" by Christopher Columbus, who thought he had reached India when he actually discovered the Caribbean Islands in 1492. The history of Native Americans is deeply linked with American expansionism.

CULTURAL DIFFERENCES

Historians are unsure how many Native Americans inhabited North America in the early 1600s, when the first permanent British **colonies** were established. Estimates vary from 1 million to 5 million people. Most native peoples were organized into tribes, groups of people who spoke the same language and had the same culture and beliefs. Most tribes made their living by hunting and fishing and practicing **subsistence agriculture.** Because of this, many native tribes migrated around the regions in which they lived. Native American tribes practiced **animistic** religions, believing in spirits of various types throughout nature.

Native tribes in North America were far less advanced than the European settlers they encountered. There were no cities like those in Europe. Native Americans had never seen a horse until they encountered Spanish explorers, because horses had become extinct in the Americas. Nor had Native Americans developed gunpowder weapons. Native Americans used bows, clubs, spears, and other such weaponry. In addition, Native Americans did not have the same concept of land ownership as did Europeans.

Cultural Exchanges Native American tribes along the East Coast introduced European settlers to a wide range of foods they had never seen. Maize (corn), squash, beans, maple syrup, sunflowers, artichokes, sweet potatoes, and avocados were all given by Native Americans to settlers. Turkeys, moose, and raccoons were all new to Europeans. Native Americans also imparted geographical knowledge to settlers and helped them survive on many occasions.

In return, Europeans passed onto the native tribes numerous devastating diseases that were unknown in North America. Diseases such as measles and smallpox decimated entire tribes, killing hundreds of thousands of native people, and weakening resistance to outside pressure from the white settlers. Settlers quickly learned that Native Americans had little knowledge of strong liquors such as whiskey and rum. Many treaties were

An essential part of the expansion of the United States was the building of railroads, which not only connected the eastern and western parts of the nation but also made transportation and shipping easier and cheaper. However, rail lines were built through Native American lands with no regard for the local people.

signed by drunken chiefs who unknowingly gave away tribal lands to outsiders.

WESTWARD EXPANSION

As the original thirteen colonies became more populated, colonists began to push west in search of cheap land on which to settle. As the United States grew, westward expansion became a common theme in American history. As a result, conflict with Native American tribes was inevitable. White settlers adopted a **racist** attitude toward Native Americans, whom they considered inferior human beings. Whites often signed treaties with native tribes, and then ignored them when given the opportunity. One historian has estimated that between 1784 and 1871 the United States signed 710 treaties with Native Americans, purchasing 2 billion acres of land. The Native Americans received little in return.

Ongoing Fighting Throughout the formation and expansion of the United States, the same process occurred over and over again. Whites would sign treaties with Native Americans. Other whites would ignore the treaties, and conflict would result. Troops would attack and defeat the native tribes, who would then be forced to sign another treaty by which they would lose more land to white settlers. By the mid-1880s, most tribes had been defeated and their land confiscated by the expanding United States. Tribes would occasionally win a battle, but white settlers so outnumbered Native Americans that they never had a chance to halt white expansion.

EARLY CONFLICTS

From the time of **colonization** until the independence of the United States, there were frequent wars with Eastern Native American tribes. During the French and Indian War (1754–1763), the French and British enlisted the aid of Native American tribes, who proved to be the real losers in this war for control of North America. Because the Native Americans practiced subsistence agriculture, it became standard practice throughout American history for soldiers or **militia** to raid their villages and fields, burning crops and warehouses. This resulted in starvation for many tribes, further weakening their resistance to whites. During the American Revolution (1775–1783), tribes aided both sides. The powerful Iroquois Confederation split, with two tribes fighting for the colonists and four aiding the British. The same situation occurred during the War of 1812 (1812–1814), when tribes again aided both sides.

DEVELOPING GOVERNMENT POLICY

As a result of the bloody conflicts with Native American tribes such as the Creek, Shawnee, and Chippewa during the War of 1812, the U.S. government began to develop a policy to lessen the chance of conflict as the nation kept expanding westward. Seizing an idea brought up by earlier presidents, Andrew Jackson (1829–1837) decided that native tribes should be moved west of the Mississippi River to prevent conflict and allow the country to grow peacefully. Congress passed the Indian Removal

Act in 1830. Under the terms of this act, the government negotiated treaties with several tribes, purchased their land, and forced them to move west of the Mississippi to what is now Oklahoma. In particular, the five "civilized" tribes in the South (Creek, Cherokee, Chickasaw, Choctaw, and Seminole) were coerced into selling their lands and moving west. Only the Seminole, based in Florida, resisted. The result was America's longest Indian war (1835–1842) and the final defeat of the Seminole, most of whom were forcibly removed from their homeland.

The government established the Bureau of Indian Affairs (later called the Indian Office) in 1824 to consolidate all government contacts with Native Amcricans under one office. A subsidiary of the War Department, the office was staffed with white Americans who often knew very little about the tribes with which they came into contact.

HISTORY MAKERS

Andrew Jackson and the Trail of Tears

The seventh president, Andrew Jackson (1829–1837), is often hailed as the president of the "common man." Indeed, he came from a poor family and was the first president elected from west of the Appalachian Mountains. Much of his early life is characterized by a rugged military career. He engaged in at least 13 duels and carried a bullet in his chest for the rest of his life. He remained popular among white citizens throughout his presidency.

President Jackson, however, is also remembered for his intense disregard of Native Americans and their rights. In May 1830, Jackson signed the Indian Removal Act into law. This law gave Jackson the power to deal with Native Americans, exchange their land for property west of the Mississippi, and remove the native peoples from American states. Jackson soon began applying pressure on the tribes to sell their land to the government and move across the Mississippi River to what is today Oklahoma.

Beginning in May 1838, soldiers rounded up about 3,000 Cherokee. Their march westward covered about 1,000 miles (1,609 km), and the Cherokee were forced to leave during the worst summer drought in 10 years. The hot, dry weather, as well as the cheating from contractors who were supposed to provide food and supplies along the way, resulted in only 1,813 Cherokee reaching Oklahoma. Thousands of Cherokee men, women, and children died en route to their new home. Bodies were buried in shallow graves. Indeed, the sorrowful trek has become known as the Trail of Tears, one of the saddest chapters in the history of the United States.

TREATIES

In 1851, the government invited 10,000 Native Americans from tribes that inhabited the Great Plains to a council at Fort Laramie. Each tribe that attended was asked to select one chief to represent the entire tribe. The resulting treaty called for whites and Indians to live in peace forever.

Broken Promises No matter how many treaties were signed between Native Americans and the United States, most were broken for various reasons. One of the main problems was the prevalent attitude among whites that Indians were inferior beings who stood in the way of progress. Also, the discovery of gold on Native American territory always precipitated a rush of **prospectors** into the area, in spite of any existing treaties. A prime example is the fate of the Shasta tribe of northern California. Gold was discovered on their land in 1850. Problems immediately erupted as conflict broke out between whites and the Shasta. In 1851, 13 chiefs and their followers accepted an invitation to meet with government representatives to sign a treaty and move off the disputed land. The white hosts prepared a feast for the Shasta, complete with poisoned meat. Thousands died, after which whites ran amok through Shasta villages, killing and burning. "That the war of extermination will continue to be waged until the Indian race becomes extinct, must be expected," wrote California governor Peter Burnett.

RESERVATIONS

As government Indian policy continued to evolve, many officials came to believe that all tribes should be placed on reservations, territory reserved especially for Native American tribes and that would be protected from white encroachment. It was also hoped that, by being restricted to a particular piece of land, tribes would settle down, give up their former migratory way of life, and become farmers. As tribes settled down, they would become more like white Americans. Many state governments established boarding schools for Native American children in an effort to educate them in white ways and influence future generations of Native Americans to act more "white."

POST–CIVIL WAR EXPANSION

Thanks to the 1862 Homestead Act, white settlement vastly increased after the Civil War. Increased conflict with Native American tribes resulted. Between 1865 and 1891, there were 13 major military campaigns against Native Americans, which resulted in more than 1,000 engagements. The Regular Army bore the brunt of these expeditions, suffering casualties of 2,006 men killed and wounded. According to one tally, Native Americans lost 4,571 killed and 1,279 wounded.

More Warfare The first major conflict, from 1866 to 1867, was a war with the Sioux over increased use of the Bozeman Trail into the Montana Territory. A treaty in 1868 ended the conflict; the trail was abandoned in return for a specific demarcation of Sioux territory. Warfare against the Cheyenne, Arapaho, Kiowa, and Comanche on the southern plains took place from 1868 to 1869.

As that war ended, President Ulysses S. Grant (1869–1877) in 1869 announced a new Indian policy. Those Native Americans willing to live peacefully on reservations would be respected as they transformed themselves into Christian farmers. "A sharp and severe war policy" would be enacted against all hostile Indians. Grant established a new Board of Indian Commissioners to coordinate government policy. Two years later, Congress passed the Indian Appropriations Act, under which all Native American tribes would no longer be considered as independent nations with the right to negotiate treaties with the United States. From now on, Congress would dictate policy to Indians without their input or approval.

Sioux Wars A major war with the Sioux erupted in 1876 when whites encroached on Sioux territory because of a gold discovery in South Dakota's Black Hills. Bands of Sioux hunting off their reservation, together with railroad construction, also contributed to this war. The historic battle took place on June 25–26, 1876, when Sioux warriors overwhelmed Lieutenant Colonel George A. Custer and most of the 7th U.S. Cavalry at the Little Bighorn, where Custer and all his men were killed. Though they won this battle, the Sioux lost the war and were forced to submit to reservation life.

In 1877, part of the Nez Perce tribe refused to move off their ancestral land and were pursued more than 1,700 miles (2,736 km) through the Rocky Mountains before surrendering to the army. A Ute war in 1879 was followed by conflict with the Apache in the Southwest. By the mid-1880s, most tribes had been defeated and forced onto reservations.

END OF NATIVE WAYS

In 1887, Congress passed the General Allotment Act, better known as the Dawes Act. It required reservation tribes to divide land among tribal members in 160-acre (64-hectare) parcels and sell all surplus land to white settlers. This law was expected to control the tribes and make them American citizens. In practice, bribery and corruption led to the sale or theft of more than 90 million acres (36,421,707 hectares) of land to whites, approximately 60 percent of remaining Native American land. Also in 1887, the Indian Bureau passed a regulation that required all Native American children to attend school. It was hoped that by doing so children would more readily identify with the white way of life.

Finally, in 1924, Congress passed a law giving citizenship to all Native Americans, although several states refused to do so. The Indian Reorganization Act of 1934 (sometimes called the "Indian New Deal") provided money for economic development, the expansion of their landholdings, and cultural preservation. Many tribes voted to reject the act and reorganize. Native Americans spent much of the twentieth century trying to recover from centuries of oppression and the attempts to force them to join mainstream American culture.

See also: California Gold Rush; Oregon Country; Seminole War.

FURTHER READING

O'Brien, Gregory. *The Timeline of Native Americans*. Berkeley, Calif.: Thunder Bay Press, 2008.

Kessel, William B., and Robert Wooster, eds. *Encyclopedia of Native American Wars and Warfare*. New York: Facts On File, 2005.

Nichols, Roger L. *American Indians in United States History*. Norman: University of Oklahoma Press, 2004.

Waldman, Carl. *Atlas of the North American Indian*. New York: Facts On File, 2009.

Northern Mariana Islands

Group of Pacific islands that became an American **trust territory** after World War II, and then a **commonwealth** associated with the United States. Spanish navigator Ferdinand Magellan was the first European to visit this group of islands, landing on Guam in 1521. Magellan called the islands "Las Islas de las Velas Latinas" (The Islands of the Latine Sails), named after the triangular shape of the sails used by native Chamorro islanders on their canoes. After fighting occurred because of theft of some of his shipboard property, Magellan referred to the islands as "The Islands of the Thieves." In 1668, their name was changed to Las Marianas in honor of Mariana of Austria, widow of Emperor Philip IV of Spain.

The United States received the island of Guam as part of the peace treaty after the Spanish-American War (1898). Spain sold the rest of the Northern Marianas to Germany in 1899. During World War I (1914–1918), Japan became a member of the Allied nations and declared war on Germany for the purpose of taking over German colonies. Japanese troops occupied the Northern Marianas, and in 1919, the League of Nations temporarily entrusted the islands to Japan.

Japan withdrew from the League of Nations in 1935 and treated the islands as its own property. After Japan attacked the United States in December 1941, Japanese troops quickly occupied Guam and turned this island, together with Saipan, Tinian, and Rota, into fortresses to contest any U.S. attack. The United States came into the Marianas in overwhelming force in June 1944. American Marines landed on Saipan on June 15, covered by the United States Fifth Fleet. The Imperial Japanese Navy steamed to attack, but in the Battle of the Philippine Sea (June 19–21), American planes destroyed more than 400 Japanese aircraft and sank three aircraft carriers, against a loss of only 30 American planes. American troops destroyed the Japanese **garrison** on Saipan by July 13. Guam was retaken by August 10 and Tinian by August 2. These islands then became airbases for long-range American bombers to attack Japan itself. The B-29 bomber that dropped an atomic bomb on Hiroshima took off from Tinian.

The new United Nations (UN) awarded the Northern Marianas to the United States to administer as part of the Trust Territory of the Pacific Islands. While most of the islands

M–N

decided to seek independence, the people of the Northern Mariana Islands voted to become a commonwealth that remained associated with the United States, an act that was approved in 1972. In January 1978, the Northern Marianas became self-governing. In November 1986, American citizenship was given to native islanders. The U.S. House of Representatives enacted a 2008 law by which the Northern Marianas could elect a representative who could vote in committee but not on the House floor.

Although there are 15 islands in the Northern Marianas, only Saipan, Tinian, and Rota have permanent residents. Threat of volcanic activity on some of the northern islands restricts habitable locations on those islands. Together, the islands total 179 square miles (46,360 hectares) with a population of more than 69,000 people.

See also: Guam.

FURTHER READING

Farrell, Donald A. *History of the Northern Mariana Islands*. Commonwealth of the Northern Mariana Islands Public School System, 1991.

Northern Mariana Visitors Authority. Available online. URL: http://www.mymarianas.com.

O–R

Oregon Country

Territory in the northwest corner of the present-day continental United States which was contested among four countries before being divided in the 1840s. The peaceful settlement of the Oregon question was a major diplomatic victory for the United States and a key part of fulfilling the nation's **manifest destiny**.

HISTORY

Early Spanish and Russian explorers first visited the coastal areas of present-day Oregon and Washington, followed by the British and Americans. Captains James Cook (1778) and George Vancouver (1792), both British explorers, explored the Pacific coast, as did American captain Robert Gray (1792) and the Lewis and Clark expedition (1805). Spain gave up its claim in 1819 when it settled the boundary issue with the growing United States, while Russia yielded its claim to the region in the 1820s.

Trappers and Traders British fur trappers and traders from the North West Company penetrated the Oregon Country early in the nineteenth century. This company was later swallowed up by the larger Hudson's Bay Company, which by the early 1840s had more than 3,000 employees in the region. American entrepreneur John J. Astor had established Astoria near the mouth of the Columbia River in 1811 as headquarters for his American Fur Company. When the War of 1812 (1812–1814) started, Astor sold his small town to the British to avoid having it captured. The peace treaty ending the war gave Astoria back to the United States.

Sharing Oregon The Oregon Country was understood to include all the territory west of the **Continental Divide** between the 42nd parallel of latitude north to the latitude 54°40′, a territory of about half a million square miles. In 1818, as part of the boundary settlement between Great Britain and the United States, the northern border of America was set along the 49th parallel from the Lake of the Woods (in present-day Minnesota) west to the crest of the Rocky Mountains. To avoid problems with deciding on how to divide the rest of the Oregon Country, American and British negotiators agreed to allow joint occupation for 10 years. In 1828, the joint occupation was extended indefinitely.

Future negotiations centered on the land north from the Columbia River to the 49th parallel. Americans wanted all of this territory and also Puget Sound, which provided one of the best natural harbors on the entire West Coast of North America. As late as 1841, however, there were only about 500 American citizens living in the Oregon Country. They were concentrated in the Willamette Valley area, near a northward-flowing **tributary** of the Columbia River.

MISSIONARIES

American missionaries journeyed to Oregon to spread Christianity to Native American tribes. Their reports of the fertile land in the Willamette Valley quickly spread across the United States. The economic downturn known as the Panic of 1837 and its financial consequences influenced many Americans to think about moving west in search of land in Oregon. A trickle of immigrants left Missouri and trekked across the Great Plains and through the Rocky Mountains in search of Oregon. The route taken became the famous Oregon Trail, a 2,000-mile-long (3,219-km) track across the continent to the Willamette Valley. In 1842, an unofficial census revealed that there were now 825 Americans in the Oregon Country. In May 1843, by a vote of 52-50, American settlers and English retirees from the Hudson's Bay Company voted to establish a temporary government to manage the growing territory.

Securing Oregon James K. Polk (1845–1849), the Democratic presidential candidate, won the 1844 election by campaigning as an **expansionist**. Polk wanted to both occupy Texas and take control of the Oregon Country, thereby expanding American influence in North America.

American expansionists bragged that they would take the entire Oregon Country, up to the southern border of Alaska. They used the popular slogan, "Fifty-four Forty or Fight!" Polk, however, was willing to settle for far less territory. The Hudson's Bay Company played into American hands by abandoning its forts and trading posts in the vicinity of the Columbia River and moving its center of operations to Vancouver Island. The influx of Americans had displaced fur-bearing animals and forced the company to move its bases.

Final Agreement As a result of more Americans and fewer fur-bearing animals, the British and American governments easily worked out an agreement to divide the Oregon Country along the 49th parallel. The northern border of the United States was simply extended west to the Pacific Ocean but excluded Vancouver Island, which remained British territory. The Senate ratified the treaty in June 1846. Oregon passed peacefully into the United States.

See also: Oregon Trail; Whitman, Marcus and Narcissa.

FURTHER READING

Merk, Frederick. *History of the Westward Movement.* New York: Alfred A. Knopf, 1978.

Nugent, Walter. *Habits of Empire: A History of American Expansion.* New York: Alfred A. Knopf, 2008.

Oregon Trail

During the 1840s and through the 1860s, major route west from Missouri to the Oregon Territory. Although there were other routes that pioneers took to the Pacific coast of the future United States before the coming of the railroads, the Oregon Trail was *the* primary route.

ORIGINS OF THE TRAIL

Americans had first visited the Pacific Northwest in the 1790s. The Lewis and Clark expedition went through the area in 1805–1806, followed by fur traders seeking beaver pelts to fuel the clothing fashions of the time. Hearing reports about the Native American tribes in the area, Protestant missionaries began to enter Oregon in the 1830s. Their stories, as well as the reports spread eastward by **mountain men** and fur traders,

increased American awareness of the settlement potential of the Oregon Territory. By the early 1840s, American settlers were beginning to brave the 2,000-mile (3,219-km) journey from Missouri to Oregon. Most settled near the Willamette River, a **tributary** of the larger Columbia River.

DANGERS OF THE TRAIL

Men, women, and children who dared to travel the Oregon Trail faced many dangers and hardships. The distance alone was a major obstacle. Most settlers who went on the trail journeyed as organized groups called wagon trains. Families banded together and chose a leader. There was strength and safety in numbers. At first, Native American tribes along the route were not a concern, but as more and more wagon trains headed west across their land, tribes would often attack the settlers, who circled their wagons at night and posted sentries to prevent surprise attacks. More often, Native Americans would shadow a train and try to run off cattle or horses so they could capture them. Many tribes would demand trades to allow settlers to pass through their land.

The weather was another major concern. Wagon trains would leave Missouri in late spring. If a wagon train left too early, there would be insufficient grass and food for the horses, oxen, and mules pulling the wagons and taken along for food. If a wagon train left too late, it would encounter the dreaded heavy snowstorms in the Rockies. If this happened, a wagon train could be

Major Trails West

Settlers of the American West used several dangerous trails to reach their new homes. Pioneers encountered rough terrain, raging rivers, harsh weather, and wild animals. Also, Native Americans, who were protecting their homelands, often attacked the pioneers' wagon trains and stole the settlers' cattle.

stranded for days or weeks and perhaps run out of food and water. A typical wagon train would take as long as six months to reach Oregon.

Fording rivers often proved to be hard work. The name of the Platte River comes from the French word for "broad, shallow, and flat," which the stream was most of the time. Melting snow from the Rockies, however, could result in a deep river impossible to cross. Many of the rivers encountered along the way had high banks, forcing the early travelers to search for places easier to cross. Many streams also contained areas of **quicksand** that could be deadly for those unlucky enough to encounter such places.

Buffalo herds were yet another danger. Numerous eyewitness accounts describe the horror felt by wagon trains that encountered herds of thousands of buffalo. A stampede could destroy or seriously damage a wagon train. Any wagon train nearing such large herds had to be very cautious and be prepared to fight for its survival.

IMPORTANCE OF THE TRAIL

The Oregon Trail was a major route west between 1843 and 1867. Perhaps as many as 350,000 people used the trail, with the peak year being 1852, when around 50,000 settlers headed west along the trail. One historian has estimated that 17,000 of these travelers died from sickness and disease, starvation, accidents, and Native American attacks. Still, the majority of travelers reached Oregon and California and helped expand the United States.

See also: Oregon Country.

FURTHER READING

Blashfield, Jean F. *The Oregon Trail*. Mankato, Minn.: Compass Point Books, 2001.

Dary, David. *The Oregon Trail: An American Saga*. New York: Alfred A. Knopf, 2004.

McNeese, Timothy. *The Oregon Trail: The Pathway to the West*. New York: Chelsea House Publishers, 2009.

Panama Canal

Completed in 1914 by the United States, channel across the Isthmus of Panama in Central America. U.S. interest in a water route across the narrow **isthmus** grew during the nineteenth century as the nation grew from sea to sea. A ship traveling from New York to San Francisco had to steam 14,000 miles (22,530 km) around Cape Horn at the southern tip of South America. A canal would reduce the miles to 6,000 (9,656 km).

When the United States learned of British interest in Central America for the same reason, Secretary of State John Clayton negotiated a treaty in 1850 that promised cooperation between the two countries if a canal was built. American investors built a 55-mile- (89-km-) long railroad across the isthmus to ease the flow of gold from California to the East Coast.

FRANCE FIRST

France was the first nation to attempt a canal across Panama, then a province of Columbia. Ferdinand-Marie de Lesseps, the engineer who built the Suez Canal in Egypt (opened 1869) took on the project but had to give up in failure. The central hills on the isthmus meant that the canal could not be a sea-level canal like the Suez. More than 20,000 laborers died, victims of tropical diseases carried by mosquitoes, and the company went bankrupt in 1889.

The Spanish-American War (1898) accelerated U.S. interest in Panama. The battleship *Oregon* steamed from California to Cuba in 68 days, pointing out the military need for a canal now that the United States had possessions in the Pacific Ocean. The first step was to negotiate a treaty with Great Britain, which was done in 1901. The British gave up their interest in a canal and thus the United States was free to seek canal rights.

The second step was to acquire the bankrupt French company's rights if the Panama route was to be chosen. There was a competing route across Nicaragua, which meant a longer canal but easier acquisition rights. However, the French company hired an American lawyer to **lobby** on its behalf. William N. Cromwell was successful because he used a Nicaraguan postage stamp that showed an active volcano to sway support his way. In 1902, the Senate voted for Panama and paid the defunct French company $40 million.

It remained for the United States to persuade Colombia to allow the canal. President Theodore Roosevelt's (1901–1909) secretary of state, John Hay, negotiated a treaty by which the United States would lease a strip of land in which to build a canal. Although the U.S. Senate **ratified** the treaty, Colombia did not.

Roosevelt then encouraged a Panamanian rebellion against Colombia. There had long been a developing Panamanian nationalism, which Roosevelt's government encouraged, with the assistance of the French company's agent, Philippe Bunau-Varilla, who helped arrange the revolt that began on November 3, 1903. On that day, Panamanian leaders declared a republic that was independent of Colombia. A U.S. warship appeared to "protect" American citizens. Colombian soldiers were bribed by U.S. supporters to stand aside, and the United States recognized the new country on November 6.

Now that Panama was independent, Secretary of State Hay negotiated a canal treaty with Panama, which was represented by Bunau-Varilla. The treaty gave the United States a 10-mile- (16-km-) wide canal zone and guaranteed that the United States would protect Panamanian independence and pay $10 million to Panama upon ratification of the treaty, then $250,000 annually. Although Panamanian leaders objected to this treaty, Hay and Bunau-Varilla had already signed it; both countries ratified the treaty in February 1904.

CONSTRUCTION BEGINS

Canal construction began in May 1904. The first vessel steamed through the canal on August 15, 1914. Rising tensions between the United States and Panama eventually led President Jimmy Carter (1977–1981) to sign a treaty with Panamanian president Omar Torrijos on September 7, 1977, preparing the way for the United States to transfer ownership of the canal to Panama. In return, Panama then signed a treaty guaranteeing the permanent neutrality of the canal.

Then&Now

Governing the Canal

From 1903 to 1979, the Panama Canal Zone was fully controlled by the United States, which had built the canal and financed its construction. During U.S. control, the territory, apart from the canal itself, was used mainly for military purposes. However, approximately 3,000 American civilians, called "Zonians," made up most of the permanent residents. In 1999, U.S. military use ended when the Zone was returned to Panamanian control.

Beginning in 1903, the Panama Canal Zone was an unincorporated U.S. territory. Almost immediately, for constitutional purposes, questions arose as to whether the Zone was considered part of the United States. In 1901, the U.S. Supreme Court had ruled that unincorporated territories, while controlled by the United States, are not *the* United States. Later, in 1904, a U.S. treasury official stated, "While the general spirit and purpose of the Constitution is applicable to the zone, that domain is not a part of the United States within the full meaning of the Constitution and laws of the country."

This situation meant babies born in the Zone were not U.S. citizens. Instead, they were considered U.S. nationals, subject to American laws but not eligible to vote, even if they moved to the states. In 1937, Congress finally passed legislation which declared that individuals born in the Canal Zone after February 26, 1904, with at least one U.S. citizen parent, were indeed U.S. citizens.

During U.S. control, the Panama Canal Zone was governed by the Canal Zone government, but the canal itself was run by the Panama Canal Company. Everyone worked for the Company or for the government. There were no independent stores; all items brought into the Zone were sold at stores run by the Company. The Zone even had its own police force, courts, and judges.

With the signing of the Torrijos-Carter Treaties, a bi-national transitional Panama Canal Commission ran the Zone from 1979 to 1999, with an American leader for the first decade and a Panamanian administrator for the second. The transition from U.S. to Panamanian control was very smooth. By 1996, more than 90 percent of the canal employees were Panamanian citizens.

Panama assumed full control on December 31, 1999.

Further Reading

Dutemple, Lesley A. *The Panama Canal.* Minneapolis, Minn.: Lerner Publishing, 2002.

Friar, William. *Portrait of the Panama Canal.* Portland, Ore.: Graphic Arts Center Publishing Company, 2003.

McCullough, David. *The Path Between the Seas: The Creation of the Panama Canal.* New York: Simon & Schuster, 1977.

Philippines

Group of Pacific Ocean islands acquired by the United States from Spain as a result of the Spanish-American War (1898). The acquisition of the Philippines by the United States was a major step in the nation's expansion of its authority and power in the Pacific region.

EARLY HISTORY

Spanish navigator Ferdinand Magellan had been the first European to sight the Philippine Islands in 1521. The islands, numbering more than 7,000, became a Spanish colony in 1565. Like many of its other colonies, the Philippines caused problems for Spain's declining empire when a Filipino revolt in favor of independence broke out in 1896. The revolt ended in 1897 when rebel leaders accepted a cease-fire in return for **exile**.

AMERICA ENDS SPANISH RULE

When it became apparent that conflict with Spain might begin soon, Commodore George Dewey, commander of the U.S. Navy's Pacific Squadron, was ordered to leave Japan and steam to Hong Kong to await further orders. On April 24, 1898, two days after the Spanish-American War began, Dewey received orders to steam to Manila Bay in the Philippines and capture or destroy the Spanish warships there. During the Battle of Manila Bay on May 1, Dewey's squadron sank all seven Spanish ships.

More than 40,000 Spanish troops still controlled the islands, and the War Department quickly began sending transport vessels filled with American soldiers across the Pacific. The first arrived near Manila on June 30. Also present was Emilio Aguinaldo, the primary Filipino rebel leader. The United States brought Aguinaldo back from Spanish-imposed exile in Hong Kong to the Philippines to organize the resistance to help the Americans against the Spanish. In return, the Filipinos expected the United States to grant them independence.

Once Manila was surrounded by American troops and Filipino **guerrillas**, the Spanish governor decided to surrender, but only to the Americans. After secret negotiations, the Spanish fought a sham battle on August 13, and then surrendered. The American commanders kept Aguinaldo's soldiers from occupying the Philippine capital. Relations between the Filipinos and Americans continued to decline, especially after word reached the Philippines that the peace treaty ending the war gave the islands to the United States in return for $20 million.

WAR IN THE PHILIPPINES

President William McKinley (1897–1901) was unsure about what to do with the Philippines. McKinley, like most Americans, had no idea where the islands were located. The president refused to allow Germany, France, or Great Britain to take over the islands. McKinley was ignorant of the islands and their people, whom he believed were incapable of governing themselves.

More realistically, the president hoped to use the Philippines as a stepping stone to open China to U.S. trade. The Senate ratified the peace treaty in February 1899, voting narrowly to keep the Philippines rather than give the islands independence.

Once word reached the Philippines that the islands were now U.S. property, relations deteriorated rapidly. On February 4, 1899, the Filipinos began a revolt against U.S. military occupation. This revolt lasted through 1902 and was a bloody, ugly conflict. Aguinaldo's troops were pushed away from Manila easily, and then resorted to guerrilla warfare, tying down thousands of American troops. By the time the war ended, more than 126,000

American soldiers had been shipped to the Philippines. They lost more than 7,000 killed and wounded. Perhaps 20,000 Filipinos were slain, with another 200,000 dead from disease and the effects of the war on local villages, crops, and farm animals.

AFTERWARD

President McKinley appointed a civilian administration, under the leadership of future president William H. Taft in July 1901. The new governor began establishing schools, improving public health, and allowing local government. In 1907, the first elections involving local candidates and political parties were held. Congress passed the Jones Act in 1916, which established a Filipino legislature but retained an American governor. The Jones Act promised future independence after a stable government was made. In 1934, the Tydings-McDuffie Act specified independence in 12 years. The Republic of the Philippines became a reality in 1946.

See also: Guam; Spanish-American War.

FURTHER READING

Morga, Antonio de. *History of the Philippine Islands*. Lenox, Mass.: Hard Press, 2006.

Nadeau, Kathleen. *The History of the Philippine Islands*. Westport, Conn.: Greenwood Press, 2008.

Polk, James K. (1795–1849)

Eleventh president (1845–1849) of the United States, largely responsible for U.S. expansion during the nineteenth century. The Mexican-American War (1846–1848), which occurred under Polk's watch, led to much of the expansion during this period.

POLITICAL LIFE

Polk's aspirations for power were helped by his marriage to Sarah Childress, daughter of a prominent Tennessee landowner. She was ambitious, charming, and well educated, and therefore an excellent match for James. Her social graces helped him gain influence as a politician, as Polk himself was considered austere and difficult to like. It was through Sarah that James became friends with presidents Andrew Jackson (1829–1837) and Franklin Pierce (1853–1857), as well as the wife of John C. Calhoun.

From 1825 to 1839, Polk served as a representative from Tennessee in the House of Representatives. During that time, he was made Speaker of the House and strongly supported the policies of President Jackson. Polk left the House to become governor of Tennessee, but he returned to Washington after he lost the 1841 and 1843 elections for governor.

THE "DARK HORSE"

In 1844, Polk attended the Democratic National Convention to try to obtain the nomination for vice president. Much to his surprise, and the surprise of many others, he was nominated instead for president. The party had been divided, and Polk was considered a compromise candidate, the first **dark horse** candidate the country had seen.

Polk took many strong stances during his campaign. Other nominees largely avoided the question as to whether the independent nation of Texas should be annexed. Polk declared that Texas should be added to the Union. He also advocated adding the entire territory of Oregon to the United States, denying Great Britain's claim on the land. The slogan "Fifty-four Forty or Fight" was a call for the border of Oregon to be set at the 54th parallel, at the southern border of Alaska.

Polk won the 1844 election. While he did tackle the Oregon issue, it was not resolved the way his campaign had promised. Rather than setting the Oregon border at the 54th parallel, a treaty with Britain set it at the 49th parallel. His plan to annex Texas resulted in the Mexican War (1846–1848). The United States claimed Texas extended to the Rio Grande, while Mexico claimed it extended only to the Nueces River. In order to solidify his claim, Polk ordered the military to march south to the Rio Grande. The Mexicans considered this an invasion, and war began. The war gained the United States not only Texas but also the Southwest and California.

After only one term, Polk left the White House. The country had been sufficiently expanded. Its borders stretched from one ocean to the other, and manifest destiny, the belief that the United States was ordained to expand and civilize the frontier, had been realized. Polk died on June 15, 1849.

See also: Lincoln, Abraham; Mexican War.

FURTHER READING

Borneman, Walter R. *Polk: The Man Who Transformed the Presidency and America.* New York: Random House, 2008.

Pony Express

Fast mail service that linked California and Missouri for 18 months in 1860 and 1861. Although the Pony Express was only a brief footnote in American history, later storytellers have elevated the riders to mythic status. The Pony Express helped the cause of expansionism by bringing news from the Eastern states to California and other parts of the American West.

ORIGINS

The idea for an express mail service that would link the East and West coasts stemmed from a conversation between California senator William Gwin and businessman William H. Russell in 1859. Russell was a business partner in the firm of Russell, Majors & Waddell, a freighting business centered in Leavenworth, Kansas. The business hauled army supplies to western posts and owned many of the wagons and teams carrying freight on the Santa Fe Trail. The firm also had a stagecoach line that went west to Salt Lake City in the Utah Territory.

Senator Gwin complained that mail from the eastern United States took so long to reach California. Although there was an existing mail route, which looped south from Missouri to El Paso, Texas, then up to Santa Fe, New Mexico Territory, and then across the desert to southern California, this route was 2,700 miles (4,345 km) long, and mail traveled very slowly, often taking months.

A French-Canadian trader named Francis Xavier Aubery was the

The first Pony Express rider left St. Joseph, Missouri, on April 3, 1860, heading west to California. Although the Pony Express lasted only about 18 months, the service has grown to be a symbol of American pride and ingenuity.

inspiration for the Pony Express. In the early 1850s, this man of daring had ridden from Santa Fe to Independence, Missouri, in only two weeks, a trip that wagons hauling goods along the Santa Fe Trail would take two to three months to do. Then, to win a $1,000 bet, Aubery, changing horses every 100–200 miles, made the trip in 5 days, 13 hours. Aubery slept for 20 hours after he collapsed at the end of his feat, but he proved that man and horse could cover great distances in a short time.

GETTING READY

Before such a service could start, Russell, Majors & Waddell had to invest a great deal of money to purchase the right type of ponies. The firm spent up to $200 each for the fastest ponies. A rider later recalled: "Sometimes we used to say that the company had bought up every mean, bucking, kicking horse that could be found, but they were good stock and could outrun anything along the trail."

Hiring Riders The firm also ran newspaper advertisements looking for suitable riders. These men often earned more than $100 per month, a princely sum in those days of low wages. A March 1860 advertisement in a San Francisco newspaper included the following description:

Wanted—young, skinny, wiry fellows, not over eighteen. Must be expert riders, willing to risk death daily. Orphans preferred. Wages $25 a week.

One historian determined that the average age of the 80 Pony Express riders was 19, with a weight of 100 to 120 pounds. The men carried only essential items, including a rifle or revolver for protection, to keep the weight down.

Setting up Stations

While riders and animals were being gathered, the firm established stations 12 to 15 miles apart, depending on the terrain. Each station consisted of a building that housed relief riders and a separate stable for horses. Riders would change horses at each station so that fresh horses could keep up the pace of around 8–10 miles per hour. Each rider would cover 75–100 miles, and then be replaced by a fresh man. The line of stations from Sacramento, California, to St. Joseph, Missouri, was divided into five sections. Each section had a supervisor responsible for keeping each station fully staffed and stocked with fresh horses. At its height, the Pony Express employed more than 200 men and had 500 horses.

PONY EXPRESS IN ACTION

Johnny Frey was the first Pony Express rider to leave St. Joseph, Missouri, at 7:15 P.M. on April 3, 1860. After 11 days, a rider reached San Francisco, California, at 12:38 A.M. on April 14. Several different men had covered a distance of 1,900 miles (3,058 km) during that time, using 75 different ponies. The route went west from St. Joseph through the present-day states of Missouri, Kansas, Nebraska, Colorado, Wyoming, Utah, Nevada, and California.

Mail Service

At first, mail went east and west once a week, every Tuesday. Each rider carried a specially designed mail pouch called a mochila. It was locked to prevent any tampering or theft. Each station master had a key for one of the pouches, which contained a timetable on which the station master entered the time that the pouch arrived at his station. Mail was limited to 10 pounds per rider. A half-ounce letter cost five dollars. To save weight, letters were written on tissue paper. As time went on, the cost per letter was reduced to less than one dollar. Mail also included private telegrams and copies of Eastern newspapers.

Dangers on the Trail

Riders took an oath of loyalty and duty to the company. They could never turn back under any circumstances. If a horse were injured or killed, the rider was to keep going on foot as fast as he was able. His main defense was the speed and endurance of his fast pony. Native Americans who occasionally interfered with the route soon found that their horses were unable to keep up with the express riders. Riders encountered packs of prowling wolves they had to outrun, swerved to avoid herds of buffalo, and coped with extreme heat and cold.

In May 1860, the two men at Williams Station in southern Nevada Territory were found slain and the station burned to the ground. The local Paiute Indians were blamed; a party of citizens went out to attack them, but were ambushed and almost wiped out. The army was called in and drove off the Native Americans and built Fort Churchill to provide better protection for the area. Pony Express service was disrupted by this brief conflict from May until early July. To make up for the interruption, riders began carrying mail twice a week.

END OF THE PONY EXPRESS

On June 16, 1860, the U.S. Congress passed the Pacific Telegraph Act, a law that provided federal money to help build a telegraph line that spanned the continent. This line was completed on October 24, 1861, and was fully operational in November. The Pony Express ceased operations on October 26, 1861, its service unable to compete with telegraph technology and speed. According to one source, the Pony Express had carried 34,753 pieces of mail on between 308 and 330 trips. The express was never profitable and was a main cause in the collapse of Russell, Majors & Waddell a short time later.

The story of the Pony Express would be lost to history except for men like William F. Cody, better known as Buffalo Bill. Often thought to be a former Pony Express rider (he was not), Buffalo Bill's Wild West Show, performing throughout the United States and Europe between 1883 and 1916, always told the epic story of the men who rode fast ponies, thus ensuring that their story would not be forgotten.

See also: California; Native Americans.

FURTHER READING

Corbett, Christopher. *Orphans Preferred: The Twisted Truth and Lasting Legend of the Pony Express.* New York: Broadway Books, 2003.

McNeese, Timothy. *The Pony Express.* New York: Chelsea House Publishing, 2009.

Moody, Ralph. *Riders of the Pony Express.* Lincoln, Neb.: Bison Books, 2004.

Popular Sovereignty

Political term meaning "rule by the people" and a major issue during the debate over slavery in the United States. Popular sovereignty is based on the idea that the people of a country have the political authority to run that country. Americans thus operate their government because they elect its officials, who serve the people and pass laws that benefit all the people.

SLAVERY AND THE TERRITORIES

The idea that popular sovereignty could solve the divisive issue of the expansion of slavery into new territories surfaced during the 1840s. Before that time, Congress had assumed the responsibility for deciding whether any new territory would include the right to own slaves, in accordance with Article IV, Section 3, of the U.S. Constitution. In 1820, Congress had enacted the Compromise of 1820 to allow Missouri to come into the Union as a slave state, but the compromise also prohibited slavery in any new territory north of Missouri's southern border.

The Mexican-American War (1846–1848) escalated the arguments over slavery in territories.

Northern members of both the Whig and Democratic parties believed that Southerners had started the war simply to grab more land in which to expand slavery. Northerners wanted slavery excluded from any territory taken from Mexico. Southerners argued that Congress had the power and responsibility to regulate the territories and protect slavery. They believed that slaves were property and that their owners should be able to take their property into any territory without fear of confiscation.

Territorial Decision Making In 1848, Michigan senator Lewis Cass proposed that Congress transfer the issue of slavery to each territorial legislature to decide. Because these legislatures were elected by the people, Cass's proposal meant that the people of each territory would decide the slavery issue. Popular sovereignty seemed to offer the solution that would end the slavery argument. However, Cass never specified how this process would work.

Kansas and Nebraska In 1854, Democratic senator Stephen A. Douglas of Illinois advanced the popular sovereignty idea during the debate over the organization of the Kansas and Nebraska territories. Douglas introduced a bill that created both territories and repealed the Missouri Compromise, allowing every new territory that would be organized to decide the slavery issue for itself. The senator hoped that popular sovereignty would remove the slavery issue from Congress and end the sectional bickering.

Douglas believed that both Kansas and Nebraska would be settled by Midwestern farmers, but after the bill was passed, proslavery settlers from Missouri moved into Kansas in an attempt to keep Kansas open to slavery. Other Missourians, called "Border Ruffians," crossed into the Kansas Territory simply to cast an illegal ballot or just to wreak havoc on antislavery settlers. Civil war broke out in "Bleeding Kansas" and lasted from 1854 until 1861. The passage of the Kansas-Nebraska Act in 1854 and its effects led to the collapse of the Whig Party, the creation of the Republican Party, and the splitting of Democrats into sectional wings. Douglas, who had hoped to be nominated for president in 1860, saw his chances to win the race dwindle. Popular sovereignty did not solve the differences over the expansion of slavery into the newly acquired territories. Indeed, it worsened the conflict.

See also: Douglas, Stephen A.; Kansas-Nebraska Act; Mexican-American War; Slavery.

Further Reading
McArthur, Debra. *The Kansas-Nebraska Act and Bleeding Kansas in American History*. Berkeley Heights, N.J.: Enslow Publishing, 2003.

Puerto Rico

Caribbean island discovered by Christopher Columbus in 1493 on his second voyage for Spain and taken by the United States from Spain during the Spanish-American War (1898). The acquisition of Puerto Rico was a major step that furthered U.S. expansion into the Caribbean region.

COLONIAL UNREST

By the mid-nineteenth century, Cuba and Puerto Rico remained Spain's last possessions in the Western Hemisphere. The developing criollo (native) culture had produced several leaders who began to clamor for more rights. Some even advocated independence from Spain. In November 1897, criollo leaders and Spanish officials reached a compromise. The two sides signed an agreement under which elected Puerto Rican representatives would become voting members of the Spanish parliament. Puerto Ricans would also have the power to create the island's budget as well as fix **import** and **export** duties. This new constitution could not be amended "except by virtue of a law and upon the petition of the insular parliament."

American Takeover

However, before these changes could take effect, the Spanish-American War began in April 1898. On July 25, American soldiers landed on the south coast of Puerto Rico at the port of Guánica. More troops went ashore at Ponce on July 27–28, followed by another landing at Arroyo on August 3.

American Occupation

Puerto Ricans were not pleased with a year of American military occupation. The war had disrupted the island's economy, which was further damaged by a severe 1899 hurricane. Coffee was the major crop in Puerto Rico at this time. Once the war was over, Spain imposed a high **tariff** to keep this product out of Spain, and the U.S. Congress failed to eliminate its own prewar tariff that kept Puerto Rican coffee from competing in the American market.

AN AMERICAN COMMONWEALTH

In April 1900, Congress passed the Foraker Act, which made the island an unincorporated American territory, meaning that the island was not eligible for statehood. Puerto Ricans became citizens of their own island, not the United States. They continued to pay export and import duties, which were returned to the island's treasury. Sugar became the island's cash crop for the next several decades, but the crop had to be refined in the United States.

Puerto Rican leaders began to seek independence, but the U.S. Congress would not allow it. In 1917, the islanders were granted American citizenship under the Jones Act as a way to counter the independence movement. The Jones Act also allowed the island to have an elected **bicameral** legislature. A 1947 law allowed the island's governor to be popularly elected. However, the president of the United States could **veto** any law with which he disagreed. Agitation on the part of Puerto Ricans led in 1952 to the changing of the island's political status to that of a **commonwealth**. Puerto Ricans may not vote in presidential elections because of the territorial status of the island.

See also: Cuba; Guam; Philippines; Spanish-American War.

FURTHER READING

Fernandez, Ronald, Serafin M. Mendez, and Gail Cueto. *Puerto Rico Past and Present: An Encyclopedia.* Westport, Conn.: Greenwood Press, 1998.

Worth, Richard. *Puerto Rico in American History.* Berkeley Heights, N.J.: Enslow Publishing, 2008.

Roosevelt, Theodore

See Panama Canal; Spanish-American War (1898).

Russia

See Alaska.

S–T

Sacajawea

See Lewis and Clark Expedition.

Santa Anna, General

See Mexican-American War (1846–1848).

Santa Fe Trail

Early trade route between Missouri and the Spanish province of New Mexico that led to a relatively easy American conquest of the region during the Mexican-American War (1846–1848). The Santa Fe Trail also provided a direct pathway for American settlers moving west as the nation expanded.

EARLY NEW MEXICO

The New Mexico province was an isolated northern outpost of Spanish culture in North America. It was hundreds of miles north of Chihuahua, the closest Spanish city. Because of strained relations with the United States, largely due to Spanish outrage over Napoleon's sale of Louisiana to the United States, Spanish officials forbade trade with the United States. Americans straying into Spanish territory were routinely seized and either imprisoned or sent back across the border.

Mexico revolted against Spanish rule and became independent in 1821. By that time, a few bold American traders had made the attempt to travel from Missouri on an 800-mile (1,287-km) journey to Santa Fe to establish trade relations and make money. In 1822, William Becknell was the first man to successfully arrive in Santa Fe and return with Mexican goods. Only a few groups of traders made the long trek across what was mistakenly labeled on early maps as the "Great American Desert." Travelers endured scorching heat in the summer and blizzards in the winter.

MOVING INTO HOSTILE TERRITORY

Native American tribes in the area were often hostile, either stealing from traveling parties or attacking them directly. American merchants joined together in large parties and took along armed guards to forestall attacks by the Osage, Kiowa, Cheyenne, Arapahoe, Pawnee, Ute, Apache, and Comanche. To move goods across this unfriendly land, men rode horses and used wagons pulled by mules, horses, or oxen.

The Trail's Route The Santa Fe Trail started in western Missouri, at the city of Independence, which was established in 1827. It then went westward across the Kansas prairies to the Great Bend of the Arkansas River, and up this river into present-day Colorado. It wound south through the mountains to Ratan Pass, then south across New Mexico to Santa Fe. Along the way, traders had to learn where to cross the many rivers they encountered, many of them with steep banks and patches of **quicksand**.

U.S. ACQUISITION OF SANTA FE

During the Mexican-American War (1846–1848), Colonel Stephen W. Kearny led U.S. troops down the trail and captured Santa Fe without any resistance on August 18, 1846. The years of contact with American merchants, coupled with distance from Mexico City, opened the door for an easy conquest of New Mexico. The Santa Fe Trail continued to be used after the war, but as more Americans moved into the area, Native Americans became increasingly hostile, and trade required even more military protection than before. The trail continued as a trade route until 1880, when the Atchison, Topeka and Santa Fe Railroad linked Santa Fe into the growing American railroad system.

See also: Louisiana Purchase; Mexican-American War; Native Americans; Oregon Trail.

During the early months of the Mexican-American War (1846–1848), U.S. Colonel Stephen W. Kearny captured the Mexican outpost of Santa Fe, New Mexico. Reaching the trading center on August 18, 1846, Kearny met with no resistance from the local people.

FURTHER READING

Blashfield, Jean F. *The Santa Fe Trail.* Mankato, Minn.: Compass Point Books, 2001.

Dary, David. *The Santa Fe Trail: Its History, Legends, and Lore.* New York: Penguin Books, 2002.

Simmons, Marc. *The Santa Fe Trail.* Lawrence: University Press of Kansas, 1986.

Scott, General Winfield

See Mexican-American War (1846–1848).

Seminole War

Conflict between the Seminole tribe of Florida and the United States in the period from 1817 to 1858, by which time the Native Americans had been defeated and most survivors moved from the territory. The U.S. successes in the Seminole War allowed the nation to settle the present-day state of Florida.

The Native Americans of Florida were composed of a series of allied tribes. The name "Seminole" is a corruption of the Spanish word *cimarrones*, which means "wild ones" or "runaways." The tribe also included "Black Seminole," descendants of fugitive slaves from the United States who intermarried with Native Americans.

The Seminole Wars were a series of three conflicts between the United States and the Seminole. The First Seminole War took place in 1817–1818. After border raids into Georgia and Alabama by the Seminole, General Andrew Jackson launched an invasion of Spanish Florida to punish the Native Americans, seizing Spanish forts in the process and creating an international incident.

After Spain **ceded** Florida to the United States in 1819, American settlers were slow to move into Florida because of the Seminole. The Native Americans were angered by white **encroachment** into their lands. U.S. efforts to move the tribe west of the Mississippi, a result of the 1830 Indian Removal Act, were largely unsuccessful. Crop failure and a wild game shortage influenced individual Seminoles to begin raiding American homesteads, and in late 1835, the Second Seminole War began.

SECOND SEMINOLE WAR

The Second Seminole War (1835–1842) turned out to be the U.S. Army's longest conflict with Native Americans, as well as one of the costliest. U.S. forces suffered 1,507 men killed. The conflict started with the Dade Massacre on December 28, 1835, when Seminole warriors surprised two companies of American soldiers and wiped them out, leaving only three wounded survivors.

Seminole raids led to a near abandonment of the Florida Territory by most whites, fearful for their lives. The **guerrilla war** waged by small bands of Seminole utterly stymied the American army. Using the swampy, wooded terrain of central and southern Florida to their advantage, the Seminole, though losing several small engagements, managed to elude the Americans.

The war continued to drag on until General Walker K. Armistead began summer attacks on the Seminole, a tactic not practiced by his predecessors because of the hot, humid weather. By August 1842, most Seminole had been captured and taken to join their tribal relatives west of the Mississippi River. The survivors were allowed to settle in southern Florida.

THIRD SEMINOLE WAR

A Third Seminole War took place from 1855 to 1858, again a result of white encroachment on Seminole lands. By the time it was over, perhaps only 150 Seminole remained in Florida. The thousands of Seminole who live in present-day Florida are descendants of these survivors. Once the Seminole threat ended, settlers quickly moved into Florida, which was admitted to the Union as a state in 1845.

See also: Florida.

FURTHER READING

Meltzer, Milton. *Hunted Like a Wolf: The Story of the Seminole War*. Sarasota, Fla.: Pineapple Press, 2004.

Missall, John, and Mary Lou Missal. *The Seminole Wars*. Gainesville: University of Florida Press, 2004.

Powers, Thomas. *Osceola: Seminole War Leader*. Lakeville, Conn.: Quercus Corporation, 1989.

Seward, William H. (1801–1872)

American politician and secretary of state for both Abraham Lincoln (1861–1865) and Andrew Johnson (1865–1869). Seward negotiated the purchase of Alaska from Russia, greatly expanding U.S. territory.

POLITICAL LIFE

Seward was elected to the New York state senate in 1830. He served there for four years. Around this time, the Whig Party started gaining power, and Seward joined the growing movement. As a Whig, Seward was elected governor of New York in 1839. Seward became strongly opposed to slavery after a trip he and his family took to the South in 1835. As governor, he resisted the call from Southern states to send back escaped slaves.

"CONSCIENCE WHIGS"

The Whig Party was divided on the slavery issue. Despite his strong anti-slavery position, Seward still supported Zachary Taylor (1849–1850), a Whig slave owner, for president. When Seward was elected to the Senate in 1848, he became leader of a **faction** of the Whig Party known as the Conscience Whigs. Seward was vocal in his moral opposition to slavery, a position that put him constantly at odds with Southern senators. Seward foresaw the eventual clash of the Northern and Southern economic systems, though he did not support war in order to force either side to accept or reject slavery.

After the collapse of the Whig Party, Seward became a Republican. He was considered a front-runner for the 1860 presidential election, but the nomination went to Abraham Lincoln instead. Lincoln had supported Seward's nomination; after Lincoln won the presidency, he appointed Seward as his secretary of state. Although Seward served President Lincoln (1861–1865) admirably throughout the Civil War (1861–1865), Seward's most memorable act as secretary of state came after Lincoln's assassination, when Seward served in President Andrew Johnson's (1865–1869) cabinet. In 1867, Seward's negotiations resulted in the purchase of Alaska from Russia.

Seward had always supported expansion of the country's borders and influence. To that end, he arranged the purchase of Alaska from Russia in

1867. The final price for Alaska was $7.2 million, roughly two cents an acre. Despite the exceedingly low price, Americans considered the purchase a mistake. In the press, the Alaska purchase was called "Seward's Folly" and "Seward's Icebox." The purchase was Seward's last major act as secretary of state. He died on October 10, 1872.

See also: Alaska.

FURTHER READING

Kent, Zachary. *William Seward: The Mastermind of the Alaska Purchase.* Berkeley Heights, N.J.: Enslow Publishers, 2001.

Slavery

System of human bondage, practiced in America from the early 1620s until 1865, when the Thirteenth Amendment to the Constitution **abolished** the practice. The issue of slavery was directly tied to the growth and expansion of the United States, as Southern slaveholders sought to take their "property" with them into any territories that the nation acquired.

HISTORY

A Dutch ship carrying about 20 Africans landed at Jamestown, Virginia, in 1619. These first Africans were treated as **indentured servants**, working to pay for their passage for a period of years and then given freedom. Soon, however, Africans were being treated differently, and slave ships began regular deliveries to the British **colonies** in North America. In 1641, Massachusetts became the first colony to legalize African slavery, which spread to every other colony over the next few decades.

Slavery proved to be more profitable in the South than in the North. Warmer southern weather was more conducive to crops such as tobacco, rice, and cotton, which all required much labor to plant and harvest. In the North, colder weather meant a shorter growing season, while the land itself was better suited to smaller farms that an owner and only a few farmhands were able to manage. The rising prices of slaves also meant that large plantations or farms were more economically profitable for their use.

SLAVERY IN THE EARLY UNITED STATES

The American Revolutionary War (1775–1783) created the United States as an independent country. From the beginning, though, there were disagreements about the status of slavery within a nation whose Declaration of Independence stated that "all men are created equal." When a convention gathered in Philadelphia to create a constitution for the United States, Northern and Southern delegates argued heatedly about slavery. Several members wanted to abolish slavery because it clearly conflicted with American ideals, but Southern members threatened to leave if slavery was ended.

Constitutional Protection As written, the U.S. Constitution protected the individual's property. Slaves were considered property and not counted as citizens. A **compromise** allowed a slave to be counted as three-fifths of a white person for purposes of state representation in the House of Representatives. The Constitution also included a clause that said the importation of slaves from outside the United States would be prohibited after 1808.

The Northwest Ordinance of 1787 prohibited slavery in the territory from which the states of Ohio, Michigan, Indiana, Illinois, Wisconsin, and part of Minnesota were created. Most Americans were **racists** who believed that African Americans were inferior human beings. The 1787 law was simply meant to protect white laborers from unfair competition from slaves.

SLAVERY AND U.S. EXPANSION

Most slaves in the early years of the United States lived in the Southern states. By the early 1800s, Northern states had begun to **emancipate** their slaves when it became apparent that slavery was not economically sound. In the South, though, slavery suddenly expanded thanks to Eli Whitney, whose invention of the cotton gin in 1793 allowed a slave picking cotton to separate seeds with ease.

The amount of cotton grown by the South made it one of the world's major cotton producers. The desire to expand the cotton crop across the lower South helped fuel the drive to remove Native American tribes from their lands and force them to move west across the Mississippi River, allowing American civilization and slavery to expand. As the United States grew, politicians in Washington, D.C., tried to maintain a balance between North and South by ensuring that when new states were admitted to the Union, there would be an equal number of slave and free states.

ABOLITIONISM AND EXPANSION

As Northern states freed their slaves, an **abolition** movement began. **Abolitionists** hoped to completely end slavery in the United States. Quakers were early leaders in this movement, as were social reformers, free blacks, and escaped slaves. Many abolitionists wished to free the slaves and send them back to Africa. Some truly believed in the equality of the races, but most were united in their belief that slavery was incompatible with the ideals upon which America was founded.

Dozens of antislavery societies were founded across the North. In 1833, the first national society, the American Anti-Slavery Society, was established in Philadelphia. By the 1850s, an active organization known as the Underground Railroad—a system of secret hiding places and safe houses to protect runaway slaves—was in place across the North as sympathetic people aided and hid escaped slaves from their owners.

SLAVERY AND THE TERRITORIES

The question of how far slavery would be allowed to expand reached national attention in 1819, when the Missouri Territory legislature petitioned Congress for admission as a state that included slavery. Heated debates in Congress centered on whether or not slavery would be allowed in the new state. The Compromise of 1820, also known as the Missouri Compromise, ended the debate by admitting Missouri as a slave state and Maine (which had been a part of Massachusetts) as a free state, keeping the balance between slave and free states. This law also specified that slavery would not be allowed in any future territory north of a line drawn from the southern border of Missouri west to the Pacific Ocean.

The issue of slavery, however, never disappeared from the national scene. As abolition societies multiplied in the North, citizens began petitioning Congress to abolish slavery. As attacks on the immorality of slavery increased, Southerners became more and more defensive. Between 1836 and 1844, thanks to the power of Southern congressmen, a gag rule went into effect that prohibited antislavery petitions from being brought before Congress.

The Slavery Question in Texas When Texas became independent from Mexico in 1836, Southerners advocated **annexing** Texas to allow slavery to spread westward. Presidents Andrew Jackson (1829–1837), Martin Van Buren (1837–1841), and William Henry Harrison (1841) all failed to act on Texas annexation because of Northern opposition. President John Tyler (1841–1845) signed an annexation treaty just before he left office. His successor, James K. Polk (1845–1849), was an **expansionist** who eagerly steered the United States into the Mexican-American War (1846–1848) to grab as much territory as possible, pushing the boundaries of the United States to the Pacific Ocean.

Wilmot Proviso Pennsylvania representative David Wilmot introduced the "Wilmot Proviso" an amendment to an **appropriations bill** in 1846. This amendment stipulated that slavery would not be allowed in any territory taken from Mexico. Although Wilmot's amendment was defeated, it rallied a large number of antislavery crusaders behind it, especially people who believed that the South was responsible for the war in an attempt to spread slavery. Significantly, the vote defeating the amendment was cast along sectional, rather than party, lines.

ARGUMENTS ESCALATE

When the region of California sought admission as a free state, the slavery debate in Congress intensified. Another compromise was reached—the Compromise of 1850. California was admitted as a free state, the slave trade was abolished in the District of Columbia, the new territories of Utah and New Mexico were organized, and a tough new fugitive slave law was enacted.

In 1854, Democratic senator Stephen A. Douglas of Illinois introduced legislation that would organize the new territories of Kansas and Nebraska and allow the residents of both territories to decide for themselves whether or not to allow slavery. In effect, Douglas's bill would repeal the Missouri Compromise and allow all future territories to vote on the slavery issue. Douglas called this idea "popular sovereignty"; the concept increased tensions in both the North and South. Northerners were furious that Douglas's bill would overturn the Missouri Compromise, while Southerners knew that slavery would not be economically sound in colder climates.

Fighting in Kansas The Kansas-Nebraska Act immediately set off a civil war in Kansas, as proslavery and antislavery agitators moved to Kansas to help sway the vote for statehood their way. In addition, some proslavery Missourians came to Kansas simply to cast an illegal ballot in an attempt to make Kansas a slave state. More than 200 people died during the fighting that erupted across Kansas between 1854 and 1861. Presidents Franklin Pierce (1853–1857) and James Buchanan (1857–1861), who were both proslavery, did little to settle the issue, but Kansas did not join the Union as a free state until January 1861.

ONGOING DIVISION

The issue of slavery in the territories was the center of national attention in the 1850s. The arguments over this issue led to the creation of the Republican Party in July 1854 and the splitting of the Democrats into Northern and Southern wings. The Supreme Court's decision in *Dred Scott v. Sandford* (1857) further alienated many Northern Democrats who felt that the Court, dominated by Southerners, had schemed to destroy Northern laws that protected both free blacks and escaped slaves. Other incidents, such as the publication of Harriet Beecher Stowe's powerful novel *Uncle Tom's Cabin* (1852) and the physical attack by South Carolina representative Preston Brooks on

Massachusetts senator Charles Sumner (May 19, 1856), contributed to the increasing split between North and South over the slavery issue.

By the time of the 1860 presidential election, both North and South had exaggerated opinions of each other that were only partly true. The spread of slavery into the territories was the major point of contention that helped bring about the Civil War (1861–1865).

See also: Douglas, Stephen A.; *Dred Scott* Case; Kansas-Nebraska Act; Popular Sovereignty; Wilmot Proviso.

FURTHER READING

Farmer, Alan. *The American Civil War: Causes, Course, and Consequences, 1803–1877 (Access to History series)*. New York: Oxford University Press, 2008.

Horton, James Oliver, and Lois E. Horton. *Slavery and the Making of America*. New York: Oxford University Press, 2005.

Spanish-American War (1898)

Brief but important conflict that resulted in the emergence of the United States as a world power. As a result of the war, the United States expanded its territories in the Caribbean region, across the Pacific Ocean, and to the Philippine Islands off the coast of Asia.

The war between Spain and the United States was the result of Spanish problems on the island of Cuba, a large Caribbean island that Columbus had discovered in 1492. U.S. interest in the island began long before the Civil War (1861–1865), when many Southerners wanted to seize the island to extend slavery. After the 1860s, American money helped the island's sugar industry grow to become Cuba's most important **export**.

BACKGROUND OF THE CONFLICT

Spain retained control of Cuba even as its other possessions slipped away. Cuban rebels fought against Spanish rule in a 10-year war from 1868 to 1878, and then again starting in 1895. This fighting disrupted U.S.-owned sugar plantations. It also caused widespread American sympathy for the rebels against the harsh military measures undertaken by Spanish general Valeriano Weyler. U.S. newspaper publishers William R. Hearst and Joseph Pulitzer printed pictures of alleged Spanish atrocities, aided by the drawings of artist Frederick Remington.

President William McKinley (1897–1901) tried to avoid conflict with Spain and offered to **mediate** an end to the fighting. However, Cuban sympathizers stole a private letter from the Spanish ambassador to the United States and had it published; the letter mocked President McKinley. On the night of February 15, 1898, the American battleship *Maine*, which had been sent to Havana harbor to protect the nation's interests,

mysteriously blew up, killing 268 sailors. U.S. newspapers were quick to blame Spain, which insisted the explosion was an accident.

Against this rising U.S. anger, the Spanish government rejected what amounted to an **ultimatum** to end the fighting in Cuba. Angered over American **intransigence**, Spain declared war on the United States on April 23, 1898. The U.S. Congress responded with its own declaration of war two days later.

A detail of an 1898 painting by W.G. Road shows an enthusiastic Lieutenant Colonel Theodore Roosevelt leading the charge of the "Rough Riders" up San Juan Hill in Cuba during the Spanish-American War (1898). Roosevelt called the conflict, which lasted 100 days, "a splendid little war."

THE PHILIPPINES

The resulting Spanish-American War lasted only 100 days. Events moved quickly. Commodore George Dewey, commanding the U.S. Navy's Asiatic Squadron, left Hong Kong and steamed to attack the Spanish fleet in the Philippine Islands. Dewey's seven ships entered Manila Bay on May 1 and destroyed all seven Spanish ships, losing only nine men wounded during the battle. Once the U.S. land forces were ashore on Luzon island in the Philippines, they besieged the capital, Manila, which surrendered on August 13.

MILITARY OPERATIONS IN THE CARIBBEAN

The main theater of operations for the United States was in the Caribbean. A Spanish naval squadron under

HISTORY MAKERS

Theodore Roosevelt (1858–1919)

As the nation's 26th president (1901–1909), Theodore Roosevelt was a major figure in the **Progressive movement**. Roosevelt was born in 1858, the son of a wealthy merchant–banker. Home-schooled as a youth, Roosevelt was often sickly and suffered from asthma. Through hard and repeated exercise, however, he overcame his physical handicaps, graduated from Harvard, and decided on a political career.

From 1882 to 1897, Roosevelt served in the New York state legislature, as a Civil Service commissioner and as New York City police commissioner. In 1897, President William McKinley (1897–1901) appointed Roosevelt assistant secretary of the navy. Roosevelt worked to make sure that the small U.S. Navy was ready for war. When the Spanish-American War began in April 1898, Roosevelt resigned to become second in command of the 1st United States Volunteer Cavalry, better known as the Rough Riders. Teddy Roosevelt led his men in the attack on Spanish positions atop Kettle Hill, in the defenses of Santiago, Cuba, on July 1, 1898.

As a war hero, Roosevelt easily won the governorship of New York, then became President McKinley's running mate in the 1900 election. After McKinley was **assassinated** in 1901, Roosevelt became the nation's youngest president at age 42. He won reelection in 1904.

In international relations, Roosevelt preached the old African proverb "Speak softly and carry a big stick, and you will go far." The president mediated an end to the Russo-Japanese War (1904–1905) and received a Nobel Peace Prize for his efforts. He backed a Panamanian revolt against Colombia so that the United States could acquire the right to build a canal across the **isthmus** of Panama. At home, Roosevelt created the National Park Service, fought against corporate greed, and regulated railroad rates. Roosevelt's presidency ushered the United States into the twentieth century.

the command of Admiral Pasqual Cervera left Spain and headed for Cuba. Cervera's ships evaded American warships and steamed into Santiago harbor on May 18. Worried that Cervera's ships might leave harbor and attack cities along the East Coast of the United States, the War Department decided that an American land force must capture Santiago to destroy the Spanish ships.

The army's Fifth Corps, under the command of General William R. Shafter, was assigned the task of capturing Santiago. Shafter's command was composed primarily of Regular Army units reinforced by a few volunteer units. The most prominent of the volunteer units was the 1st U.S. Volunteer Cavalry, better known as the Rough Riders. Its colonel was Leonard Wood, White House physician to the president; second in command was Theodore Roosevelt, who resigned his post as assistant secretary of the navy for the chance to go into combat. In command of the American cavalry was 62-year-old Joseph Wheeler, who had been a Confederate general during the Civil War.

Shafter's command left Tampa, Florida, on June 12 and landed about 15 miles east of Santiago 10 days later. Shafter had about 17,000 soldiers to oppose roughly the same number of Spanish defenders. After some **skirmishing** as the troops advanced toward Santiago, Shafter deployed his troops and launched an attack on July 1. The fighting centered on Spanish positions at El Caney, a village near Santiago, before the main American assault on Kettle and San Juan hills.

The Rough Riders featured prominently in the successful attack on Kettle Hill, as did the African American 10th U.S. Cavalry.

However, the American occupation of part of the city's defenses meant that Cervera's ships were endangered if the Americans continued to edge closer to the harbor. So, on July 3, Admiral Cervera tried to flee the harbor. By the time the naval battle was over, every Spanish ship had been sunk or beached and set afire. Santiago surrendered on July 17.

As American and Spanish authorities began to discuss peace terms, American troops landed on the south coast of Puerto Rico and began to advance toward the island's capital, San Juan, skirmishing with Spanish troops. Much of the island was under American control when an **armistice** was announced on August 13.

THE PEACE TREATY

Peace negotiations began in Paris in late September. The peace treaty formally ending the war was signed on December 10. Spain **ceded** Cuba to the United States, with the understanding that after a brief period of occupation the island would be given independence. Spain also gave up Puerto Rico and Guam. The United States also acquired the Philippines for a payment of $20 million to Spain.

The acquisition of the Philippines was controversial. Most Americans had never heard of these faraway islands; many did not even know where they were until newspapers began printing maps of the conflict. However, President McKinley felt that the

United States could not give the islands back to Spain and allow a situation similar to Cuba to continue. After Dewey's victory in Manila Bay, German warships had appeared, followed by Japanese ships, to survey the situation. If the United States pulled out, one of these powers would surely take control of the Philippines. Thus, McKinley decided that the United States must retain them.

The Spanish-American War resulted in the acquisition of an overseas empire that few Americans could have foreseen just a few years before 1898. The new territories presented both challenges and dangers for the United States.

See also: Cuba; Philippines.

FURTHER READING

Dolan, Edward. *The Spanish-American War.* Brookfield, Conn.: Millbrook Press, 2001.

Goldstein, Donald, et al. *Spanish-American War: The Story and Photographs.* Dulles, Va.: Potomac Books, 2000.

Nofi, Albert A. *The Spanish-American War, 1898.* Conshohocken, Pa.: Combined Books, 1996.

Somerlott, Robert. *The Spanish-American War: "Remember the Maine."* Berkeley Heights, N.J.: Enslow Publishers, 2002.

States, Admission of New

Important idea that was an advanced political concept of the late eighteenth century and led to long-term political stability in the United States. When the original 13 **colonies** gained their independence from Great Britain after the Revolutionary War (1775–1783), there was much debate about the way in which the new United States would expand. The former British colonies had all been granted charters by the kings and queens of England. Many of these charters contained vague or inaccurate geographical descriptions of colonial boundaries. As a result, there were conflicting border claims that had to be settled.

WESTERN LAND CLAIMS

One of the major problems resulting from the royal charters was the conflict over the western borders of seven states. Many royal charters granted specific northern and southern boundaries that were to extend from the Atlantic to the Pacific. The 1783 Treaty of Paris placed the western border of the United States along the Mississippi River, effectively halting any border claims at that river. There were several years of delay in ratifying the Articles of Confederation because those states with no western claims wanted the states with claims to give up their western lands to the new central government. By 1792, all the states except Georgia had given up their western land claims; Georgia yielded in 1802.

THE NORTHWEST ORDINANCE

The Northwest Ordinance was enacted in 1787 and provided a plan for the growth of the Northwest Territory, the unsettled land west of Pennsylvania, north of the Ohio River, and east of the upper Mississippi River (the future states of Ohio, Indiana, Illinois, Michigan, Wisconsin, and part of Minnesota).

The Northwest Ordinance specified that no more than five territories would be carved from the larger

Northwest Territory. Each would have a territorial government (governor, secretary, and three judges) appointed by Congress. When the population reached 5,000 adult males, the territory could elect an assembly. When the population reached 60,000, the territorial assembly could petition Congress for admission as a state. Each territory would have the same rights as the original 13 states.

As the nation grew, Congress extended the provisions of the Northwest Ordinance to all lands acquired during the period of westward expansion. By allowing territories to grow and mature into states, and by using the very term *territory* rather than *colony*, Congress undercut attempts at revolution and provided for an orderly growth as new territory was added to the United States.

The adoption of the Northwest Ordinance had its opponents as well as its supporters. Opponents argued that as the West grew, so would the number of new states. The original 13 states would lose their prominence in the new nation. Opponents suggested that a limit should be set on new states so that there would never be more than 12. When the Constitution was written in 1787, a compromise was included that gave Congress the power to admit new states, but no further details were written into the document.

CONFLICTS

The extension of the principles of the Northwest Ordinance worked well over time. The major problem that was interjected into territorial expansion was the slavery issue. The admission of Missouri in 1820 led to a **compromise** to limit the spread of slavery into territories north of Missouri. The **annexation** of Texas was delayed in part because of Northern fears over the spread of slavery. In fact, the coming of the Civil War (1861–1865) was in part the result of the fighting about the issue of slavery in the territories.

See also: Kansas-Nebraska Act; Slavery; Utah Territory.

FURTHER READING

Merk, Frederick. *History of the Westward Movement.* New York: Alfred A. Knopf, 1978.

Smith, Gary A. *State and National Boundaries of the United States.* Jefferson, N.C.: McFarland & Company, 2004.

Stein, Mark. *How the States Got Their Shapes.* New York: HarperCollins Publishers, 2008.

Sumner, Charles

See Slavery.

Sutter, John

See California Gold Rush.

Texas

Province of Spanish Mexico that was coveted by American **expansionists** after the Louisiana Purchase in 1803. Many Americans, because of the vague borders of the Louisiana Territory, believed that Louisiana extended into present-day Texas. In 1819, Secretary of State John Quincy Adams negotiated the Adams-Onís Treaty, which defined the western border of the Louisiana Territory.

Although the U.S. government thus gave up any territorial claims to Texas, individual Americans continued to show an interest in Texas. Mexico became independent from Spain in 1821. Spain had always loosely administered the province, partly because of its small **tejano** population and partly because of the hostile Native American tribes occupying the area (primarily the Comanche).

THE EMPRESARIO SYSTEM

To spark interest in settling Texas, the Mexican government offered grants of huge tracts of land to anyone who would bring at least 200 families. The families brought in by each **empresario** would also receive land; the amount depended on whether the family would farm or graze animal herds. Such **immigrants** would be free from taxes for six years but had to become Mexican citizens and convert to the Catholic faith, which was the Mexican national religion. By regulating the **immigration** of foreigners into Texas, the Mexican government hoped both to populate the province and build a buffer against American expansionism.

Many Americans were eager to **immigrate** to Mexico. The Panic of 1819, a severe financial crisis, had badly disrupted the American economy. This, coupled with the United States Land Office's sale policy for federally owned territory, made the offer of free land in Mexico hard to resist. Moses Austin, a New England–born American, had lost a fortune during the Panic of 1819. Austin had applied for a Spanish land grant, which was interrupted by Mexican independence. After the death of the elder Austin, his son Stephen F. Austin was given a contract to bring families to Texas.

Austin was just one of many empresarios given contracts for land in Texas. Austin, however, emerged as one of the most prestigious empresarios, one who outwardly obeyed Mexican laws in return for his land grant. Other Americans were not so obedient to Mexico. Mexico passed laws in 1823 and 1824 that **abolished** slavery. For a while, American immigrants were allowed to bring their slaves with them, but the buying and selling of slaves in Mexico was forbidden. In 1829, slavery was abolished completely in Mexico. American settlers, however, refused to comply with the Mexican law.

OPPOSITION TO FURTHER IMMIGRATION

Mexican attempts to halt further American immigration to Texas were ineffective. By the early 1830s, more than 30,000 Americans had settled in Texas. Many of these Americans were illegal **squatters** who moved into Texas in search of free land. Lack of enforcement by the weak Mexican government failed to halt the steady stream of American settlers, most of whom refused to convert to Catholicism or become Mexican citizens. Most Americans believed that Mexicans were inferior and resented any attempts to tighten control over Texas.

History Speaks

Texas Annexation Treaty, 1845

On March 1, 1845, President John Tyler signed into law the joint resolution of Congress approving the annexation of Texas. The text that follows is Section 2 of this resolution, specifying how Texas would join the United States.

2 . . . *First*, Said State to be formed, subject to the adjustment by this government of all questions of boundary that may arise with other governments; and the constitution thereof, with the proper evidence of its adoption by the people of said Republic of Texas, shall be transmitted to the President of the United States, to be laid before Congress for its final action, on or before the first day of January, one thousand eight hundred and forty-six.

Second, Said State, when admitted into the Union, after ceding to the United States, all public edifices, fortifications, barracks, ports and harbors, navy and navy yards, docks, magazines, arms, armaments, and all other property and means pertaining to the public defense belonging to said Republic of Texas, shall retain all the public funds, debts, taxes, and dues of every kind, which may belong to or be due and owing said republic; and shall also retain all the vacant and unappropriated lands lying within its limits, to be applied to the payment of the debts and liabilities of said Republic of Texas, and the residue of said lands, after discharging said debts and liabilities, to be disposed of as said State may direct; but in no event are said debts and liabilities to become a charge upon the Government of the United States.

Third. New States, of convenient size, not exceeding four in number, in addition to said State of Texas, and having sufficient population, may hereafter, by the consent of said State, be formed out of the territory thereof, which shall be entitled to admission under the provisions of the federal constitution. And such States as may be formed out of that portion of said territory lying south of thirty-six degrees thirty minutes north latitude, commonly known as the Missouri compromise line, shall be admitted into the Union with or without slavery, as the people of each State asking admission may desire. And in such State or States as shall be formed out of said territory north of said Missouri compromise line, slavery, or involuntary servitude, (except for crime), shall be prohibited.

THE TEXAN REVOLT

Mexican general Antonio López de Santa Anna took over the Mexican government as president in 1833. Instead of restoring a federal style of government, Santa Anna became a **dictator**. In the eyes of the Americans in Texas, he launched a reign of cruelty and oppression. In July 1833, Austin went to the capital of Mexico City to explain the Texans' grievances. Santa Anna had him thrown into jail, where he remained for two years.

In the meantime, Mexican-Texan relations went rapidly downhill. Santa Anna dissolved the Mexican Congress in May 1834, and then abolished state governments in October 1835. By the time Austin returned to Texas in July 1835, American tempers were flaring. In October 1835, Texans confronted a force of Mexican soldiers and defeated them, sparking a wave of resistance across the province. Soon, all Mexican troops had been driven from Texas, which created a government that announced it was loyal to the 1824 Mexican constitution.

Santa Anna raised an army of more than 4,000 men and marched into Texas. In late February, most of his army arrived in San Antonio, where a force of 182 rebels had outfitted the old Alamo **mission** as a fort. After a two-week **siege**, the Mexicans attacked on March 6, overwhelming the **garrison**, which was annihilated. One woman and a slave were allowed to go free to report the fate of the Texans. Another Texan force of 340 men at the settlement of Goliad was surrounded and captured; the men were then executed on Santa Anna's orders.

News of the massacres led to a widespread evacuation of Texas as Americans began fleeing toward the Louisiana border. Texas declared its independence from Mexico on March 2 and appointed Sam Houston to raise an army. Houston, in spite of criticism from the newly appointed temporary government, retreated to the east as Santa Anna continued to advance. Houston finally stopped when he reached the San Jacinto River, northwest of Galveston Bay. On April 21, 1836, as Santa Anna's troops rested, Houston's 800 men attacked. Shouting "Remember the Alamo!" the sudden and furious Texan attack panicked the Mexicans, who fled in all directions. By the time the killing stopped, Houston's men accounted for the deaths of 630 Mexicans, another 208 wounded, and 730 captured, including Santa Anna. Only two of Houston's men were slain. Santa Anna then signed two **treaties** that recognized Texan independence and ended the war. Back in Mexico City, however, the government refused to accept the treaties, claiming they were signed under duress.

THE LONE STAR REPUBLIC

Texans elected Sam Houston president in September 1836. More than 90 percent of the voters also favored annexation to the United States. The new Texas constitution recognized the Rio Grande as its southern and western boundaries, with a line drawn north from the source of the Rio Grande to intersect the U.S.

boundary as indicated by the 1819 treaty with Spain.

President Andrew Jackson (1829–1837) did not quickly move to push Texas **annexation**, however. Northerners were suspicious that the Texas revolt was an attempt by slaveholders to extend slavery. To avoid fighting, Congress suggested that Jackson grant recognition to Texas as an independent country, which he did on March 4, 1837, his last day as president. President Martin Van Buren (1837–1841) also avoided annexation, which he feared would lead to war with Mexico. The Panic of 1837, a severe economic crisis, also diverted American interest away from Texas. When William Henry Harrison (1841) became president in 1841, he chose for secretary of state Daniel Webster, a Northerner who opposed Texas annexation.

While the United States deferred annexation, the Republic of Texas was facing many problems. Conflicting land claims, coupled with crooked land **speculators**, clogged the legal system. The existence of slavery in Texas made Great Britain hesitant to recognize the new country. The new government was heavily in debt and had trouble raising money even as more American immigrants continued moving into Texas in search of free land. President Mirabeau Lamar, who succeeded Houston, moved the capital from Houston to the new town of Austin, and then launched an unsuccessful attack on New Mexico, further deepening the Texas debt.

Sam Houston again became president, contending with angry Comanche warriors in western Texas,

Mexican military attacks on its border, and no money. By 1842, the British seemed willing to help. Already arguing with the United States over the Oregon Territory to the north, British diplomats saw an opportunity to embarrass the Americans by making Texas a British protectorate, abolishing slavery, and interrupting U.S. foreign trade.

ANNEXATION

When President Harrison died unexpectedly, Virginian John Tyler (1841–1845) became president. Tyler was suspicious of British interference in Texas and worried because of their stand against slavery. In 1844, Tyler appointed John C. Calhoun as secretary of state. Calhoun was very much in favor of annexing Texas and pushed Texas into agreeing to a treaty of annexation.

However, many members of the U.S. Senate, especially Northern senators, did not support Tyler's annexation idea. Calhoun had foolishly declared that Texas must be annexed to protect American slavery from British abolition, thus alienating many Northerners. Many senators also worried that annexing Texas would lead to war with Mexico. Members of the Whig Party argued that the United States should consolidate its current territory before taking even more. The Senate defeated the annexation treaty by a vote of 35-16.

Tyler waited until Democrat James K. Polk (1845–1849) won the presidential election of 1844. Polk had favored Texas annexation in his campaign, and so Tyler presented a joint resolution to Congress to annex

Texas. A joint resolution required only a simple majority to pass, unlike a formal treaty, which required a two-thirds majority. The joint resolution passed the House 120-98 and the Senate 27-25. Tyler signed it into law on March 1, 1845, three days before leaving office. In Texas, Sam Houston called for a special election to choose delegates to a convention to decide on the annexation treaty. On July 4, 1845, this convention approved annexation to the United States. Texas became the 28th state on December 29, 1845.

See also: Mexican-American War; Polk, James K.; Tyler, John.

FURTHER READING

David, William C. *Lone Star Rising: The Revolutionary Birth of the Texas Republic*. New York: Free Press, 2003.

McDonald, Archie P. *Texas, A Compact History*. Abilene, Tex.: State House Press, 2007.

Wade, Mary D. *Texas History*. Portsmouth, N.H.: Heinemann Educational Books, 2008.

Tyler, John (1790–1862)

Tenth president of the United States (1841–1845); he was responsible for successfully pushing the **annexation** of the Republic of Texas into Congress.

EARLY CAREER

Tyler was a firm defender of slavery. He voted against the Missouri Compromise (1820) because he felt that Congress could not regulate slavery by treating Missouri differently than other states. Tyler was the only legislator to vote against a law that allowed President Andrew Jackson (1829–1837) to use force against South Carolina during the **nullification** crisis of the early 1830s.

Election of 1840 William Henry Harrison, the 1840 Whig candidate for president, selected Tyler as his vice-presidential running mate. Harrison won the election but served as president for only one month before he died from pneumonia in April 1841. Tyler thus became president, the first vice president to succeed to the nation's highest office. When he **vetoed** a Whig plan for a new national bank, Tyler's cabinet resigned in protest. For the rest of his presidency, Tyler was a man without a party and an ineffectual leader.

Annexing Texas During his administration, Texas officials approached Tyler to ascertain whether or not he favored annexation by the United States. Texas had won its freedom from Mexico in 1836 and was an independent republic, but it was afflicted with economic problems and threatened by Mexico. Earlier American presidents had avoided the issue of Texas annexation because a large number of Americans opposed it. Mexico had threatened war with the United States if it annexed Texas, and most Americans did not want war. Northern abolitionists claimed that Southern advocates of slavery wanted to annex Texas so they could extend slavery and keep their political advantage in Congress.

Tyler, however, ordered his secretary of state, Abel Upshur, to negotiate a treaty of annexation with Texas. Upshur was killed in an accident on

February 28, 1844, after which Tyler appointed John C. Calhoun as his new secretary of state. Texas agreed to the treaty on April 12, 1844, but the treaty ran into serious problems in the Senate, which defeated the treaty 35-16.

Tyler Moves to Annex Texas James K. Polk (1845–1849), the Democratic candidate, won the 1844 presidential election. Polk, too, favored annexation of Texas, and Tyler saw Polk's victory as a chance to push annexation through before he left office. Tyler's final message to Congress on December 3, 1844, warned that if the United States did not annex Texas, Great Britain might take control of the republic. On January 25, 1845, both the House (120-98) and Senate (27-25) passed a resolution approving the annexation. Because a two-thirds majority was needed for success, however, this vote failed. Undeterred, Tyler had the bill resubmitted as a joint resolution, which required only a simple majority to pass, which it did. The president signed the Texas annexation bill into law on March 1, 1845, three days before Polk was sworn into office. Polk completed the annexation treaty later that year.

See also: Manifest Destiny; Texas.

FURTHER READING

Heidler, David S., and Jeanne T. Heidler. *Manifest Destiny*. Westport, Conn.: Greenwood Press, 2003.

Walker, Jane C. *John Tyler: A President of Firsts*. Granville, Ohio: McDonald and Woodward Publishing Company, 2001.

U–Z

Utah Territory

Western territory once considered one of the most isolated places in North America. Acquired by the United States under the Treaty of Guadalupe-Hidalgo (1848), which ended the Mexican-American War (1846–1848), Utah did not become a state until much later because of controversies surrounding the Mormon faith.

HISTORY

Although Spanish explorers had crossed what is now southern Utah in the 1770s, the first white man to see the Great Salt Lake was **mountain man** Jim Bridger, who moved through the region from 1824 to 1825. Competing British (from Canada's Hudson Bay Company) and American groups of fur trappers had been combing the Rocky Mountains to trap beaver and prevent the other nation from staking claim to more land. Beaver pelts were much prized in Europe and the eastern United States, because a beaver's soft underfur was used to make felt for hats then in fashion.

Spanish Rule Utah was Spanish territory until the Mexican-American War (1846–1848), after which it was transferred to the United States as part of the peace treaty. Spanish influence in the area was minimal at best, and **immigrant** wagon trains to California, as well as scouting expeditions, regularly crossed the area but never stayed because of the salt flats and desert-like conditions. U.S. army officer John C. Frémont scouted the Great Salt Lake in September 1843 and then again in 1845. His published reports came to the attention of Mormon leaders searching for a new place to live.

Mormon Migration The Church of Jesus Christ of Latter-Day Saints, commonly known as the Mormons, had begun in New York State in 1830. Because of their decision to remain aloof from the rest of society, which they considered corrupt and evil, Mormons were driven out of New York. They moved to Ohio, Missouri, and then Illinois. Joseph Smith, their founder, was murdered in 1844, after which most of the Mormons moved west to the Iowa-Nebraska border to consider where to go from there.

Brigham Young, the new Mormon leader, decided to move the Mormon community to the Great Salt Lake area. In April 1847, he and an advance

In the 1850s, Mormon pioneers ford a stream as they trek westward to Salt Lake City in the Utah Territory. The Mormons, or the Church of Jesus Christ of Latter-Day Saints, moved to the Utah Territory to avoid persecution.

party left their settlements in eastern Nebraska and moved across the Great Plains and through the Rockies, sighting the lake in July. Because of their earlier migrations through several states, Mormons had learned how to build settlements and now put their knowledge to good use by creating a new community near the lake. Young went back east in 1848 and began to send groups westward to the salt lake.

Deseret As the Mormons congregated around the Great Salt Lake, Young and other leaders declared in 1849 that they had established the state of Deseret, which encompassed all of modern Utah and Nevada and parts of California, Arizona, New Mexico, Colorado, Wyoming, Oregon, and Idaho. The name Deseret was the word for honeybee, taken from *The Book of Mormon*. Young hoped to remain separated from the United States as long as possible.

However, only a year later, as part of the Compromise of 1850, Congress created the Utah Territory, with a far smaller area than claimed by Deseret. President Millard Fillmore (1850–1853) appointed Young as the first governor of the new territory. Mormons continued to come to Utah, thanks in large part to the Perpetual Emigrating Fund Company, established in 1850 to pay transportation costs for Mormons worldwide to **immigrate** to their promised land. During the 37 years this company was in existence, it paid the costs for 85,000 immigrants.

Conflict Because Mormons valued unity and combined their church and state, federal territorial officials were ignored and often undermined by the Mormon majority. When a judge resigned and complained to President James Buchanan (1857–1861), the president ordered the army to occupy the territory and enforce U.S. law. The brief Mormon War of 1857–1858 ended without bloodshed when the Mormons allowed an army post to be established near Salt Lake City and the appointment of a non-Mormon as governor.

MOVING TOWARD STATEHOOD

Army officer Patrick E. Connor encouraged the start of silver and gold mining in Utah during the Civil War (1861–1865). This, coupled with the completion of the **transcontinental railroad** at Promontory Point, Utah, in 1869, led to a large influx of non-Mormon residents to Utah. By 1890, non-Mormons comprised 34 percent of the territory's population of 208,000.

The territory had more than enough residents to qualify for statehood, but the Mormon practice of **polygamy** horrified the rest of the country and resulted in cries to **abolish** this practice. A succession of federal laws tried to invalidate this practice, which was defended as a First Amendment right by the Mormons. In 1887, a federal law was passed that was designed to destroy the Mormon Church both economically and politically. Three years later, after another law **disenfranchised** all Mormons, church president Wilford Woodruff ordered the end of polygamy. After additional concessions by Mormon leaders, Utah was finally admitted to the Union as the 45th state in 1896.

See also: Mexican-American War.

FURTHER READING

May, Dean L. *Utah: A People's History*. Salt Lake City: University of Utah Press, 1987.

Stegner, Wallace, and Richard W. Etulain. *Mormon Country*. Lincoln, Neb.: Bison Books, 2003.

Virgin Islands

Group of Caribbean islands purchased by the United States from Denmark in 1917, during World War I (1914–1918). This purchase not only prevented the islands from possibly falling under German control, but it also expanded U.S. presence in the Caribbean region.

Located 40 miles (64 km) east of Puerto Rico, the islands were first sighted by Christopher Columbus in 1493. He named them "The Virgins" in honor of the legendary beauty of Saint Ursula and her virgins martyred during a wave of persecution of early Christians in the ancient Roman Empire.

U.S. INTEREST

The United States developed an interest in the Danish West Indies shortly after the Civil War (1861–1865). Secretary of State William Seward in 1866 traveled around the Caribbean, searching for suitable locations for naval bases and **coaling stations** for the growing American navy. Seward was interested in keeping European nations away from a proposed canal across the **isthmus** of Panama. The Danish West Indies were located on one of the main entry points into the Caribbean, and U.S. control would greatly enhance canal security.

Seward negotiated a treaty with the nation of Colombia to allow the United States to build a canal across Panama, which at the time was a province of Colombia. He found that Denmark was eager to part with the West Indies islands because the cost of upkeep exceeded the value of products the islands produced. Seward and the Danish foreign minister agreed upon a purchase price of $7.5 million and signed a treaty in 1867. The inhabitants approved **annexation** to the United States, and the Danish parliament **ratified** the treaty. However, the U.S. Senate showed no interest and allowed the treaty to lapse without voting on it.

U.S. ACQUISITION

Presidents William McKinley (1897–1901) and Theodore Roosevelt (1901–1909) both unsuccessfully tried to obtain the islands. The outbreak of World War I (1914–1918) finally persuaded the Danes to part with their West Indian islands. The Danes worried that Germany might invade Denmark and then take over Danish colonial possessions. In October 1915, President Woodrow Wilson's (1913–1921) secretary of state, Robert Lansing, informed the Danes that the United States was interested in the islands. A treaty was signed on August 4, 1916, in which the United States paid $25 million for the islands. This time, the Senate ratified the treaty on September 17. After Denmark approved the treaty, President Wilson signed it into law on January 16, 1917.

After their purchase by the United States, the islands became known as the U.S. Virgin Islands. Residents received American citizenship in 1927 and in 1971 were allowed to elect their own governor rather than have one appointed by the U.S. government. Since 1954, there have been five attempts to give islanders more control over their own affairs. Each time, though, voters have rejected more freedom because it would mean higher taxes. Today, the Virgin Islands are a magnet for tourists.

FURTHER READING

"Brief History of the Virgin Islands." Available online. URL: http://www.vinow.com.

Dookhan, Isaac. *History of the Virgin Islands*. Kingston, Jamaica: University Press of the West Indies, 2000.

Webster-Ashburton Treaty

Signed in 1842, Anglo-American treaty that settled ongoing boundary disputes between the United States and Canada. The treaty peacefully settled the dispute in the United States' favor, thus allowing the nation to devote its resources to westward expansion.

A LONG-STANDING DISPUTE

The Treaty of Paris that ended the Revolutionary War (1775–1783) included specifications about the northern boundary of the new United States, but the treaty's vague language, and the fact that the boundary was supposed to run across an area about which little was known geographically, meant that the boundary was never mapped out.

Maine became a state in 1820. As its population began to increase, settlers moved north into uncharted wilderness and swamps and came into contact with Canadians from the province of New Brunswick. Understanding that a definite boundary was needed, the United States and Great Britain submitted the problem to a **neutral** third party to resolve. The king of the Netherlands examined the situation and in 1831 divided the 12,000 square miles (3,107,985 hectares) in question equally between both countries. Although the British parliament accepted this decision, the U.S. Senate rejected it.

Compromise After a border dispute threatened to erupt into war (the so-called Aroostook War of 1838–1839), Daniel Webster, the American secretary of state under President John Tyler (1841–1845), contacted Great Britain and said the United States was willing to draw up a new treaty. The British selected Lord Ashburton as its negotiator. Ashburton was married to an American woman and was a friend of Webster's, so the two men worked together in a friendly manner to devise a new treaty.

Working from April through mid-July, the two men drew up a treaty, which both signed on August 9, 1842. Webster then worked behind the scenes to ensure that the Senate would ratify this treaty and that the American public would understand that a **compromise** was a good way to end this situation. Webster even showed Maine state officials an old map supposedly used during the Treaty of Paris negotiations, a map that favored the extreme British claim for the Maine boundary and that had been forgotten in Great Britain. The Senate voted 39-9 in favor of the treaty, which the British parliament also accepted.

TERMS OF THE TREATY

The Webster-Ashburton Treaty awarded 7,000 square miles (1,812,991 hectares) of the disputed area to the United States. The treaty also awarded $125,000 each to Maine and Massachusetts (from which Maine was created in 1820) from Great Britain.

The treaty also clarified the boundary along the St. Lawrence River, as well as the northern boundary between the present-day state of Minnesota and Canada, which had been another unsettled question since the 1803 Louisiana Purchase. The Minnesota boundary settlement continued the U.S.-Canadian border westward along the 49th parallel of longitude to the Rocky Mountains. The disputed Oregon Territory west of the Rockies would be left to a future treaty. Also included in the Webster-Ashburton Treaty was a clause promising Anglo-American cooperation to suppress the illegal African slave trade, as well as a process to **extradite** criminals between the two nations. All in all, the treaty was a friendly compromise to the American-Canadian boundary issue.

See also: Louisiana Purchase; Oregon Country.

FURTHER **R**EADING

Howe, Daniel W. *What Hath God Wrought: The Transformation of America, 1815–1848.* New York: Oxford University Press, 2007.

Stein, Mark. *How the States Got Their Shapes.* New York: HarperCollins, 2008.

Whitman, Marcus and Narcissa (1802–1847, 1808–1847)

Husband and wife and Protestant missionaries who started a **mission** in the Oregon Country, now Washington State. Their mission became a stop on the Oregon Trail, and Marcus was instrumental in establishing the Oregon Trail, used by thousands of people to settle the West.

SECOND GREAT AWAKENING

During Marcus's teen years, New England was experiencing a religious revival, known as the Second Great Awakening. Revival meetings were held in many small towns, and people came to gatherings to experience personal salvation. Church attendance skyrocketed, and Christian groups sponsored schools and other charities in the hopes of spreading God's word.

Marcus's experience with the revivals convinced him that he wanted to become a minister, though he was unsure of what denomination. At age 18, he informed his family of his decision, but they were not happy about the news. Becoming a minister required four years of college and three years of study at a seminary. The family could spare neither the money nor the labor that Marcus provided for his uncle's tannery.

In 1823, Marcus began studying to be a doctor with a local physician. In 1825, he enrolled in the College of Physicians and Surgeons of the Western District of New York at Fairfield.

That same year, Marcus got his license to practice medicine. He practiced for more than two years before again seriously considering becoming a minister. As his plan never came to be, he instead returned to medical school in 1831 to get his doctorate.

For the next four years, he practiced medicine in Wheeler, New York. In 1835, Whitman indulged his religious feelings again, this time by applying to the American Board of Commissioners for Foreign Missions. Because only married couples were allowed to be missionaries, Whitman was instead hired as a scout and doctor. He traveled with Samuel Parker to what is now Montana and Idaho, searching for suitable locations for future missions. The Flathead and Nez Perce Indians were particularly friendly to the missionaries' preaching, and Whitman vowed that he would return to teach them Christian ways.

SINGULAR MISSION

When he returned to New York, Whitman married Narcissa Prentiss. Narcissa was born on March 14, 1808, in Steuben County, New York. Like Marcus, she was greatly affected by the Second Great Awakening. When she was 11, she had a religious experience at a revival meeting that resulted in her conversion. When she was 16, she had already decided that she wanted to be a missionary. In 1834, Narcissa's family moved to the town of Amity, New York, where she heard Reverend Samuel Parker call for missionaries. The Reverend sent Narcissa's application to the Board of Commissioners for Foreign Missions.

It was a mere two months after Marcus had sent in his application.

Like Marcus, Narcissa had a strong missionary drive. Also like Marcus, the Board of Commissioners for Foreign Missions rejected her application to become a missionary because she was not married. Their marriage was, in many ways, one of convenience. It would further their life goals and allow them to go on an adventure that they would otherwise have been denied. They were married on February 18, 1836.

During their journey to Oregon Country, Narcissa became pregnant with her first and only child, Alice. She was born on March 14, 1837, but died two years later. Traveling with the Whitmans were Henry and Eliza Spalding, two missionaries bound for working with the Osage tribe. During the trip, Eliza and Narcissa became the first two white women to cross the **Continental Divide** at the top of the Rocky Mountains. It had been previously believed that women did not have the strength to cross the Rocky Mountains.

MISSION OPENS

In 1836, Marcus and Narcissa founded their mission in Waiilatpu, outside of present-day Walla Walla, Washington. There they ministered to the Cayuse Indians. Marcus taught the Cayuse how to farm. He taught them irrigation techniques and later helped build mills to grind their corn and wheat into flour. Narcissa made use of her teaching experience and set up a school. In 1842, however, the Board of Commissioners of Foreign Missions decided that progress with the Cayuse had been too slow. They wanted to abandon the mission and relocate both the Whitmans and the Spaldings to Spokane.

Marcus Whitman made the journey all the way back to Boston, Massachusetts, to convince the board to keep the missions open. Not only was he successful there, but he also then went to Washington, D.C., to inform the federal government that Oregon Country was suitable for settlement. On his journey back to Washington, Whitman helped a caravan of 1,000 settlers navigate the treacherous route.

When he returned to his mission in Waiilatpu, Whitman found that he now had competition for the Cayuse's attention. Catholic missionaries had also settled in the area, and the Cayuse found the pomp and ceremony of Catholic services attractive. Whitman was disheartened. He had determined to leave the mission when a measles epidemic broke out, brought by the white settlers who had followed him out west.

Because he was a doctor, Whitman stayed to tend to the sick. Many of the white children recovered, while many of the Indian children did not, due to a lack of natural immunity. The Cayuse, however, believed that Whitman had deliberately let their children die to weaken their numbers and take their land. They held Whitman personally responsible for the deaths, and on November 29, 1847, the Cayuse took their revenge. They attacked Whitman's home, killing both Marcus and Narcissa. Strife between the white settlers and the Cayuse continued after their deaths.

See also: Lewis and Clark Expedition; Oregon Country; Oregon Trail.

FURTHER READING

Harness, Cheryl. *The Tragic Tale of Narcissa Whitman and a Faithful History of the Oregon Trail.* Des Moines, Iowa: National Geographic Children's Books, 2006.

Jeffrey, Julie Roy. *Converting the West: A Biography of Narcissa Whitman.* Norman: University of Oklahoma Press, 1994.

Wilmot Proviso

Legislation proposed in 1846 that would have prevented slavery in all territory acquired from Mexico as a result of the Mexican-American War (1846–1848). The proviso, and the support it received in Congress, shows the interconnection of the slavery issue to the expansion of the United States.

REPRESENTATIVE WILMOT

The Wilmot Proviso's author, David Wilmot, was a Democratic member of the House of Representatives. Wilmot was born and reared in Pennsylvania and represented a district in the northern part of the state. Wilmot initially supported President James K. Polk (1845–1849) and the war with Mexico.

In August 1846, days before Congress was scheduled to adjourn until December, President Polk sent to Congress an **appropriations bill,** asking for $2 million to use essentially as a bribe to induce Mexico to make peace and allow the United States to acquire territory from Mexico in any peace treaty. On August 8, during the debate about this bill, Wilmot offered the following amendment:

Provided, That, as an express and fundamental condition to the acquisition of any territory from the Republic of Mexico by the United States, by virtue of any treaty which may be negotiated between them, and to the use by the Executive of the moneys herein appropriated, neither slavery nor involuntary servitude shall ever exist in any part of said territory, except for crime, whereof the party shall first be duly convicted.

GROWING OPPOSITION

By the time Wilmot introduced this amendment, he and many other northern Democrats had become convinced that Polk had started the war simply to extend slavery. The expansion of slavery would also lead to the continued Southern domination of the federal government that had continued since the United States first became independent. Although the House passed the bill amendment 83-64, the bill died in the Senate, which refused to consider the bill before adjourning. Wilmot offered his amendment during the next session. Again, the House passed it (115-105), but the Senate deleted the proviso from its version of an appropriations bill.

Wilmot's Motive Wilmot was *not* an antislavery agitator. He once said that he introduced the proviso to preserve the rights of white landowners. Wilmot believed that slavery, if confined to the South, would eventually die out without interference from **abolitionists**. "Slavery has within itself the seeds of its own destruction," he wrote.

Keeping Slavery out of the Territories The Wilmot Proviso opened a new era in the fight over slavery. Before Wilmot's involvement, the battle over slavery included a wide range of issues. The Wilmot Proviso rallied the antislavery crusade behind the idea of preventing slavery from spreading into new territories. The proviso split the Whig Party into Northern and Southern wings and effectively led to the party's collapse. The Democratic Party also began to split into sectional wings that would affect its ability to speak for the entire country in any national elections. The proviso also helped bring about the formation of the Republican Party, which was opposed to the spread of slavery into the new western territories.

See also: Mexican-American War.

FURTHER READING

Howe, Daniel W. *What Hath God Wrought: The Transformation of America, 1815–1848*. New York: Oxford University Press, 2007.

Morrison, Michael A. *Slavery and the American West: The Eclipse of Manifest Destiny and the Coming of the Civil War*. Chapel Hill: University of North Carolina Press, 1997.

Zone, Canal

See Panama Canal.

President Thomas Jefferson, Reasons for Purchasing New Orleans, 1802

President Thomas Jefferson (1801–1809) constantly worried about the French acquisition of the Louisiana Territory and its effects on American commerce down the Mississippi River to New Orleans. The president wrote a letter to Robert R. Livingston, the American minister to France, on April 18, 1802, outlining his concerns and suggesting that the United States purchase the New Orleans area to ensure American control of the Mississippi for its trade. Jefferson, as seen in this letter, was misinformed about Spain's Florida territory, which had not been **ceded** to France.

> " The cession of Louisiana and the Floridas by Spain to France, works most sorely on the United States. . . . It completely reverses all the political relations of the United States, and will form a new epoch in our political course. Of all nations of any consideration, France is the one which, hitherto, has offered the fewest points on which we could have any conflict of right, and the most points of a communion of interests. From these causes, we have ever looked to her as our *natural friend*, as one with which we could never have an occasion of difference. Her growth, therefore, we viewed as our own, her misfortunes ours. There is on the globe one single spot, the possessor of which is our natural and habitual enemy. It is New Orleans, through which the produce of three-eighths of our territory must pass to market, and from its fertility it will ere long yield more than half of our whole produce, and contain more than half of our inhabitants.
>
> France, placing herself in that door, assumes to us the attitude of defiance. Spain might have retained it quietly for years. Her pacific dispositions, her feeble state, would induce her to increase our facilities there, so that her possession of the place would hardly be felt by us, and it would not, perhaps, be very long before some circumstance might

arise, which might make the cession of it to us the price of something of more worth to her.

France: the impetuosity of her temper, the energy and restlessness of her character, placed in a point of eternal friction with us, and our character, which, though quiet and loving peace and the pursuit of wealth, is high-minded, despising wealth in competition with insult or injury, enterprising and energetic as any nation on earth; these circumstances render it impossible that France and the United States can continue long friends, when they meet in so irritable a position. They, as well as we, must be blind if they do not see this; and we must be very improvident if we do not begin to make arrangements on that hypothesis.

The day that France takes possession of New Orleans, fixes the sentence which is to restrain her forever within her low-water mark. It seals the union of two nations, who, in conjunction, can maintain exclusive possession of the ocean. From that moment, we must marry ourselves to the British fleet and nation. We must turn all our attention to a maritime force, for which our resources place us on very high ground; and having formed and connected together a power which may render reenforce-ment [sic] of her settlements here impossible to France, make the first cannon which shall be fired in Europe the signal for the tearing up of any settlement she may have made, and for holding the two continents of America in sequestration for the common purposes of the United British and American nations. This is not a state of things we seek and desire. . . .

If France considers Louisiana, however, as indispensable for her views, she might perhaps be willing to look about for arrangements which might reconcile it to our interests. If anything could do this, it would be the ceding to us the island of New Orleans and the Floridas. This would certainly, in a great degree, remove the causes of jarring and irritation between us, and perhaps for such a length of time, as might produce other means of making the measure permanently conciliatory to our interests. It would, at any rate, relieve us from the necessity of taking immediate measures for countervailing such an operation by arrangements in another quarter. But still we should consider New Orleans and the Floridas as no equivalent for the risk of a quarrel with France, produced by her vicinage.

On the Oregon Trail, 1843

Jesse Applegate (1811–1888) wrote a memoir about his experiences on the Oregon Trail. Applegate, born in Kentucky and a resident of Missouri, was the leader of the "cow column," a train of wagons transporting a herd of cows that slowed progress. This excerpt provides a vivid picture of what was done to get the train moving each morning.

> It is four o'clock a.m.; the sentinels on duty have discharged their rifles—the signal that hours of sleep are over; and every wagon and tent is pouring forth its night tenants, and slow-kindling smokes begin largely to rise and float away on the morning air. Sixty men start from the corral, spreading as they make through the vast herd of cattle and horses that form a semi-circle around the encampment, the most distant perhaps two miles away.
>
> The herders pass to the extreme verge and carefully examine for trails beyond, to see that none of the animals have strayed or been stolen during the night.
>
> This morning no trails lead beyond the outside animals in sight, and by five o'clock the herders begin to contract the great moving circle and the well-trained animals move slowly toward camp, clipping here and there a thistle or tempting bunch of grass on the way. In about an hour five thousand animals are close up to the encampment, and the teamsters are busy selecting their teams and driving them inside the "corral" to be yoked. The corral is a circle one hundred yards deep, formed with wagons connected strongly with each other, the wagon in the rear being connected with the wagon in front by its tongue and ox chains. It is a strong barrier that the most vicious ox cannot break, and in case of an attack of the Sioux would be no contemptible entrenchment.
>
> From six to seven o'clock is a busy time; breakfast is to be eaten, the tents struck, the wagons loaded, and the teams yoked and brought up in readiness to be attached to their respective wagons. All know when, at seven o'clock, the signal to march sounds, that those not ready to take their proper places in the line of march must fall into the dusty rear for the day.
>
> There are sixty wagons. They have been divided into fifteen divisions or platoons of four wagons each, and each platoon is entitled to lead in its turn. The leading platoon of today will be the rear one tomorrow, and will bring up the rear unless some teamster, through indolence or negligence, has lost his place in the line, and is condemned to that uncomfortable post. It is within ten minutes of seven; the corral but now a strong barricade is everywhere broken, the teams being attached to the

wagons. The woman and children have taken their places in them. The pilot (a borderer who has passed his life on the verge of civilization, and has been chosen to the post of leader from his knowledge of the savage and his experience in travel through the roadless wastes) stands ready in the midst of his pioneers, and aids, to mount and lead the way. Ten or fifteen young men, not today on duty, form another cluster. They are ready to start on a buffalo hunt, are well mounted, and well armed as they need be, for the unfriendly Sioux have driven the buffalo out of the Platte, and the hunters must ride fifteen or twenty miles to reach them. The cow drivers are hastening, as they get ready; to the rear of their charge, to collect and prepare them for the day's march.

It is on the stroke of seven; the rushing to and fro, the cracking of the whips, the loud command to oxen, and what seems to be the inextricable confusion of the last ten minutes has ceased. Fortunately every one has been found and every teamster is at his post. The clear notes of the trumpet sound in the front; the pilot and his guards mount their horses, the leading division takes up the line of march, the rest fall into their places with the precision of clock work, until the spot so lately full of life sinks back into that solitude that seems to reign over the broad plain.

President James K. Polk, Inaugural Address, 1845

In his inaugural address on March 4, 1845, President James K. Polk (1845–1849) spoke at length about his desire to **annex** both Texas and Oregon. This excerpt shows his reasoning behind **annexation**. Although some of his thinking was simply wrong (Texas was never a part of the Louisiana Purchase), his strong words influenced millions of Americans to agree with their leader's decisions to expand U.S. territory, either through war or peace. Polk clearly expressed the viewpoint of manifest destiny in this first speech as president.

> Texas was once a part of our country—was unwisely ceded away to a foreign power—is now independent, and possesses an undoubted right to dispose of a part or the whole of her territory and to merge her sovereignty as a separate and independent state in ours. I congratulate my country that by an act of the late Congress of the United States the assent of this Government has been given to the reunion, and it only remains for the two countries to agree upon the terms to consummate an object so important to both.
>
> I regard the question of annexation as belonging exclusively to the United States and Texas. They are independent powers competent to contract, and foreign nations have no right to interfere with them or take exceptions to their reunion. Foreign powers do not seem to appreciate the true character of our Government. Our Union is a confederation of independent States, whose policy is peace with each other and all the world. To enlarge its limits is to extend the dominions of peace over additional territories and increasing millions. The world has nothing to fear from military ambition in our Government. . . . Foreign powers should therefore look on the annexation of Texas to the United States not as the conquest of a nation seeking to extend her dominions by arms and violence, but as the peaceful acquisition of a territory once her own, by adding another member to our confederation, with the consent of that member, thereby diminishing the chances of war and opening to them new and ever-increasing markets for their products. . . .
>
> To Texas the reunion is important, because the strong protecting arm of our Government would be extended over her, and the vast resources of her fertile soil and genial climate would be speedily developed, while the safety of New Orleans and of our whole southwestern frontier against hostile aggression, as well as the interests of the whole Union, would be promoted by it. . . .

Captain Alfred Thayer Mahan, Reasons for a Large Fleet, 1890

Alfred Mahan (1840–1914) graduated from the U.S. Naval Academy in 1859. After many years of service at sea, Mahan lectured at the newly established Naval War College. He organized the lectures into a book, *The Influence of Sea Power Upon History, 1660–1783*, which was published in 1890. It quickly became an international hit among military strategists in Europe and Asia as well as in the United States. In this excerpt, Captain Mahan sums up the need for a **merchant marine** and **colonies**, as well as for a war fleet to protect them both.

❝ Under modern conditions, however, home trade is but a part of the business of a country bordering on the sea. Foreign necessaries or luxuries must be brought to its ports, either in its own or in foreign ships, which will return, bearing in exchange the products of the country, whether they be the fruits of the earth or the works of men's hands; and it is the wish of every nation that this shipping business should be done by its own vessels. The ships that thus sail to and fro must have secure ports to which to return, and must, as far as possible, be followed by the protection of their country throughout the voyage.

This protection in time of war must be extended by armed shipping. The necessity of a navy, in the restricted sense of the word, springs, therefore, from the existence of a peaceful shipping, and disappears with it, except in the case of a nation which has aggressive tendencies, and keeps up a navy merely as a branch of the military establishment. As the United States has at present no aggressive purposes, and as its merchant service has disappeared, the dwindling of the armed fleet and general lack of interest in it are strictly logical consequences. When for any reason sea trade is again found to pay, a large enough shipping interest will reappear to complete the revival of the war fleet. It is possible that when a canal route through the Central-American Isthmus is seen to be a near certainty, the aggressive impulse may be strong enough to lead to the same result. This is doubtful, however, because a peaceful, gain-loving nation is not far-sighted, and far-sightedness is needed for adequate military preparation, especially in these days.

As a nation, with its unarmed and armed shipping, launches forth from its own shores, the need is soon felt of points upon which the ships can rely upon for peaceful trading, for refuge and supplies. In the present day friendly, though foreign, ports are to be found all over the world; and their shelter is enough while peace prevails. It was not always so, nor does peace always endure, through the United States have been favored by so long a continuance of it. In earlier times the merchant seaman, seeking for trade in new and unexplored regions, made his gains at risk of life and liberty from suspicious or hostile nations, and was under great delays in collecting a full and profitable freight. He therefore intuitively sought at the fare end of his trade route one or more stations, to be given to him by force or favor, where he could fix himself or his agents in reasonable security, where his ships could lie in safety, and where the merchantable products of his land could be continually collecting, awaiting the arrival of the home fleet, which should carry them to the mother-country. As there was immense gain, as well as much risk, in these early voyages, such establishments naturally multiplied and grew until they became colonies; whose ultimate development and success depended upon the genius and policy of the nation from which they sprang, and form a very great part of history, and particularly of the sea history, of the world. . . . **❞**

President William McKinley, War Message to Congress, 1898

On April 11, 1898, President William McKinley (1897–1901) issued a statement to Congress reviewing the recent revolt in Cuba against Spanish rule. He also addressed the previous American attempts to end the fighting, which had been ruining American business interests on the island.

President McKinley had just received official word from Spain that American suggestions would be accepted and an end to the fighting would soon occur. However, in his message, the president presented a biased point of view, one that heaped more blame on Spain than was necessary. Spain declared war on April 23; Congress issued its own declaration on April 25. In the following excerpt, the president summed up reasons why the United States should intervene in Cuba and asked to use military force to resolve the conflict.

> Obedient to that precept of the Constitution which commands the President to give from time to time to the Congress information of the state of the Union and to recommend to their consideration such measures as he shall judge necessary and expedient, it becomes my duty now to address your body with regard to the grave crisis that has arisen in the relations of the United States to Spain by reason of the warfare that for more than three years has raged in the neighboring island of Cuba.
>
> I do so because of the intimate connection of the Cuban question with the state of our own Union and the grave relation the course which it is now incumbent upon the nation to adopt must needs bear to the traditional policy of our government if it is to accord with the precepts laid down by the founders of the republic and religiously observed by succeeding administrations to the present day.
>
> The present revolution is but the successor of other similar insurrections which have occurred in Cuba against the dominion of Spain, extending over a period of nearly half a century, each of which, during its progress, has subjected the United States to great effort and expense in enforcing its neutrality laws, caused enormous losses to American trade and commerce, caused irritation, annoyance, and disturbance among our citizens, and, by the exercise of cruel, barbarous, and uncivilized practices of warfare, shocked the sensibilities and offended the humane sympathies of our people. . . .

The grounds for such intervention may be briefly summarized as follows:

First. In the cause of humanity and to put an end to the barbarities, bloodshed, starvation, and horrible miseries now existing there, and which the parties to the conflict are either unable or unwilling to stop or mitigate. It is no answer to say that this is all in another country, belonging to another nation, and is therefore none of our business. It is specially our duty, for it is right at our door.

Second. We owe it to our citizens in Cuba to afford them that protection and indemnity for life and property which no government there can or will afford, and to that end to terminate the conditions that deprive them of legal protection.

Third. The right to intervene may be justified by the very serious injury to the commerce, trade, and business of our people and by the wanton destruction of property and devastation of the island.

Fourth, and which is of utmost importance. The present condition of affairs in Cuba is a constant menace to our peace and entails upon this Government an enormous expense. With such a conflict waged for years in an island so near us and with which our people have such trade and business relations; when the lives and liberty of our citizens are in constant danger and their property destroyed and themselves ruined; where our trading vessels are liable to seizure and are seized at our very door by war ships of a foreign nation. . . .

The long trial has proved that the object for which Spain has waged the war can not be attained. The fire of insurrection may flame or may smolder with varying seasons, but it has not been and it is plain that it can not be extinguished by present methods. The only hope of relief and repose from a condition which can no longer be endured is the enforced pacification of Cuba. In the name of humanity, in the name of civilization, in the behalf of endangered American interests which give us the right and the duty to speak and to act, the war in Cuba must stop.

In view of these facts and of these considerations, I ask the Congress to authorize and empower the President to take measures to secure a full and final termination of hostilities between the Government of Spain and the people of Cuba, and to secure in the island the establishment of a stable government, capable of maintaining order and observing its international obligations, insuring peace and tranquility and the security of its citizens as well as our own, and to use the military and naval forces of the United States as may be necessary for these purposes.

Glossary of Key Terms

abolition The act of abolishing or doing away with, as in the abolition of slavery.

abolitionist A person who supports abolition, for example, the abolition of slavery.

animist A person who holds a primitive belief that both animate and inanimate objects, such as animals and plants, have souls.

annex To add territory to an existing state or country.

annexation The addition of territory to an existing nation or state.

appropriation bill A legislative bill that specifies how public money (taxes) will be spent.

armistice A cease-fire or suspension of hostilities between two countries by the consent of both sides.

bicameral A legislature composed of two house, or branches.

cede To give control or ownership of a piece of land to another nation.

census The process of counting every inhabitant of the United States; the census takes place every ten years as specified by the Constitution.

claim jumper A person who illegally mines or inhabitants another person's property.

coaling station A military base that provides coal or other fuel for warships.

colonization The process of establishing a colony, or settlement.

colony Land settled by people from a distant country, in which the people remain loyal to their homeland after settling.

commonwealth A nation or state ruled by its people.

compromise A settlement of differences between two opposing parties in which each party makes some concessions.

Continental Divide The section of high ground throughout the Rocky Mountains where rivers and streams flow east on one side and west on the other.

coup Change of government by a sudden illegal action.

custom A tax on imported goods.

dark horse A political candidate who receives unexpected support for nomination during a political convention.

de facto A Latin term meaning "actual."

democracy A government in which the people govern themselves through elected representatives.

dictator A ruler who has supreme power over the government of a country.

disenfranchise To take away the right to vote.

emancipate To set free.

emigrate To leave one area and settle in another.

empresario A Spanish businessman; used to name those Americans who were given land grants in Spanish Texas.

encroachment The act of intruding or trespassing upon someone or something.

exile Forced banishment from one's native country.

expansionist A person who believes in enlarging his or her country's territory.

export To send or carry goods abroad for selling or trading.

extradition The legal process of sending an alleged criminal from one country or state to another for trial.

faction A minority within a larger group.

Federalist Party An early U.S. political party that favored a strong central government.

garrison A term used to describe the soldiers stationed in a city, fort, or other permanent military post.

guerrilla warfare A type of war in which one side uses small bands of soldiers or civilians to harass a superior enemy.

immigrants People who move from one country or area and settle in another.

immigration The process of moving from one country or area and settling in another country or area.

import To bring or carry goods into a country from foreign countries.

indentured servant One who signs a contract with another specifying a length of time during which the first person must work as a servant for the second person.

indigenous Of or relating to the native peoples of a region.

intransigence Refusal to budge from an extreme position in order to compromise.

isthmus A narrow piece of land between two bodies of water.

lame duck An elected official who remains in office during the period after an election and the time the next person assumes that office.

lobby Attempting to influence politicians by special interest groups.

martial law Rule by military forces.

mediate To settle a conflict between two countries by acting as a neutral agent.

merchant marine A nation's vessels that carry commerce.

militia Civilians called into military service during an emergency; in the United States, the militia eventually became the modern National Guard.

mission A religious building established in another country or area in order for religious officials to conduct charitable or religious work.

naturalization The process of acquiring full citizenship in a country.

neutral Not belonging to a side; unbiased.

nullification The action of a state in refusing to enforce federal laws within its territory.

peninsula Land bordered on three sides by water.

polygamy The practice of having more than one wife at the same time.

portage The carrying of boats and supplies between two waterways, usually done to avoid impassible sections that include rapids and waterfalls.

Progressive movement A late nineteenth, early twentieth-century political movement in the United States whose members sought to reform the government and make it more responsive to the people.

prospector A person who explores an area, looking for minerals such as gold and silver.

protectorate A relationship in which a stronger country protects and partially controls a weaker country.

quicksand A bed of loose sand mixed with water that easily sucks in anything that walks on it.

racism The belief that one race is superior to other races.

racist A person who believes his or her own ethnic group is superior to others.

ratify To confirm the wording of an official document.

reciprocity treaty A treaty between two countries that includes an exchange of terms beneficial to both countries.

reservation In the United States, a piece of land set aside for a certain group to live upon; especially used for Native American land.

revenue Income from all sources used by a government to pay its bills.

secede To break away from a country or other union.

secession The act of seceding, or breaking away.

siege A military operation in which troops surround a town or city in order to capture it.

skirmish An encounter between small bodies of troops from hostile armies.

sluice An artificial channel for conducting water that contains a valve or gate to regulate flow.

squatters People who build their homes upon land they do not own.

subsistence agriculture A method of farming in which the farmers grow only enough to feed their families.

suffrage The right to vote.

tariff A tax on goods being imported into a country.

tejano A Hispanic resident of Texas.

transcontinental railroad A railroad built to connect the East and West coasts of the United States.

treaties Formal agreements between two or more countries which contain specific terms relating to trade, boundaries, peace, alliances or related points.

tributary A smaller river that flows into a larger river.

trust territory A area of land entrusted to another country to manage until the people of that area are able to elect their own government and become independent.

ultimatum A final statement of terms sent by one party to another, usually considered a threat of what will happen if that party does not agree to the terms.

veto To reject formally, as in rejecting a proposed law.

yellow fever Caused by a virus, an infectious tropical disease that causes dark-colored vomiting and jaundice.

Ambrose, Stephen E. *Undaunted Courage: Meriwether Lewis, Thomas Jefferson, and the Opening of the American West*. New York: Simon & Schuster, 1996.

American Samoa: 100 Years Under the United States Flag. N.p.: Island Heritage, 2000.

American Samoa Historic Preservation Office. Available online. URL: http://www.ashpo.org.

Andrist, Ralph K. *The California Gold Rush*. New York: American Heritage Publishing Company, 1961.

Baker, Christopher P. *Cuba Handbook*. Chico, Calif.: Moon Publications, 2006.

Barnes, Phil. *A Concise History of the Hawaiian Islands*. Hilo, Hawaii: Petroglyph Press, 1999.

Blashfield, Jean F. *The Santa Fe Trail*. Mankato, Minn.: Compass Point Books, 2001.

"Brief History of the Virgin Islands." Available online. URL: http://www.vinow.com.

Cannavale, Matthew C. *Voices from Colonial America: Florida 1513–1821*. Washington, D.C.: National Geographic Children's Books, 2006.

Casey, Charles W. *The Mexican War: Mr. Polk's War*. Berkeley Heights, N.J.: Enslow Publishing, 2002.

Corbett, Christopher. *Orphans Preferred: The Twisted Truth and Lasting Legend of the Pony Express*. New York: Broadway Books, 2003.

Cromwell, Sharon. *Dred Scott v. Sandford: A Slave's Case for Freedom and Citizenship*. Mankato, Minn.: Compass Point Books, 2009.

Cunningham, Lawrence J., and Janice J. Beaty. *A History of Guam*. Honolulu, Hawaii: Bess Press, 2001.

Dary, David. *The Oregon Trail: An American Saga*. New York: Alfred A. Knopf, 2004.

———. *The Santa Fe Trail: Its History, Legends, and Lore*. New York: Penguin Books, 2002.

de Morga, Antonio. *History of the Philippine Islands*. Lenox, Mass.: Hard Press, 2006.

Ditchfield, Christin. *The Lewis and Clark Expedition*. Danbury, Conn.: Children's Press, 2006.

Dolan, Edward. *The Spanish-American War*. Brookfield, Conn.: Millbrook Press, 2001.

Dookhan, Isaac. *History of the Virgin Islands*. Kingston, Jamaica: University Press of the West Indies, 2000.

Dosal, Paul J. *A Brief History of Cuba*. Wheeling, Ill.: Harlan Davidson Publishing, 2006.

Dutemple, Lesley A. *The Panama Canal*. Minneapolis, Minn.: Lerner Publishing, 2002.

Farmer, Alan. *The American Civil War: Causes, Course, and Consequences, 1803–1877*. New York: Oxford University Press, 2008.

Farrell, Donald A. *History of the Northern Mariana Islands*. Commonwealth of the Northern Mariana Islands Public School System, 1991.

Feldman, Ruth T. *The Mexican-American War*. Minneapolis, Minn.: Lerner Publishing, 2004.

Finkelman, Paul. *Dred Scott v. Sandford: A Brief History with Documents*. New York: Bedford/St.Martin's, 1997.

Foster, Lynn V. *A Brief History of Central America*. New York: Facts On File, 2000.

Friar, William. *Portrait of the Panama Canal*. Portland, Ore.: Graphic Arts Center Publishing Company, 2003.

Gannon, Michael. *Florida: A Short History*. Gainesville: University Press of Florida, 2003.

Goldstein, Donald, et al. *Spanish-American War: The Story and Photographs*. Dulles, Va.: Potomac Books, 2000.

Heidler, David S., and Jeanne T. Heidler. *Manifest Destiny*. Westport, Conn.: Greenwood Press, 2003.

Horton, James Oliver, and Lois E. Horton. *Slavery and the Making of America*. New York: Oxford University Press, 2005.

Howe, Daniel W. *What Hath God Wrought: The Transformation of America, 1815–1848*. New York: Oxford University Press, 2007.

Hyslop, Stephen G. *Bound for Santa Fe: The Road to New Mexico and the American Conquest, 1806–1848*. Norman, Okla.: University of Oklahoma Press, 2002.

Isserman, Maurice. *Across America: The Lewis and Clark Expedition*. New York: Facts On File, 2004.

Joy, Mark S. *American Expansionism, 1783–1860: A Manifest Destiny?* London: Pearson Education Limited, 2003.

Kinzer, Stephen. *Overthrow: America's Century of Regime Change from Hawaii to Iraq*. New York: Henry Holt & Company, 2006.

Kluger, Richard. *Seizing Destiny: How America Grew from Sea to Shining Sea*. New York: Alfred A. Knopf, 2007.

Madden, Ryan. *Alaska: On the Road Histories*. Northampton, Mass.: Interlink Publishing Group, 2005.

May, Dean L. *Utah: A People's History*. Salt Lake City: University of Utah Press, 1987.

McArthur, Debra. *The Kansas-Nebraska Act and Bleeding Kansas in American History*. Berkeley Heights, N.J.: Enslow Publishers, 2003.

McCullough, David. *The Path Between the Seas: The Creation of the Panama Canal*. New York: Simon & Schuster, 1977.

McDonald, Archie P. *Texas, A Compact History*. Abilene, Tex.: State House Press, 2007.

McNeese, Timothy. *Dred Scott V. Sandford*. New York: Chelsea House Publishers, 2006.

McNeese, Timothy. *The Louisiana Purchase: Growth of a Nation*. New York: Chelsea House Publishers, 2008.

McNeese, Timothy. *The Oregon Trail: The Pathway to the West*. New York: Chelsea House Publishers, 2009.

McNeese, Timothy. *The Pony Express*. New York: Chelsea House Publishers, 2009.

Meed, Douglas V. *The Mexican War, 1846–1848*. New York: Routledge, 2003.

Meltzer, Milton. *Hunted Like a Wolf: The Story of the Seminole War*. Sarasota, Fla.: Pineapple Press, 2004.

Mercati, Cynthia. *Forty-niners: The Story of the California Gold Rush*. Logan, Iowa: Perfection Learning, 2002.

Merk, Frederick. *Manifest Destiny and Mission in American History*. New York: Alfred A. Knopf, 1963.

Missall, John, and Mary Lou Missall. *The Seminole Wars: America's Longest Indian Conflict*. Gainesville: University Press of Florida, 2004.

Moody, Ralph. *Riders of the Pony Express*. Lincoln, Neb.: Bison Books, 2004.

Nadeau, Kathleen. *The History of the Philippine Islands*. Westport, Conn.: Greenwood Press, 2008.

Nardo, Don. *The Mexican-American War*. Farmington Hills, Mich.: Greenhaven Press, 1999.

Nelson, Sheila. *Thomas Jefferson's America: The Louisiana Purchase, 1800–1811*. Broomall, Pa.: Mason Crest Publishers, 2005.

Nichols, Roger L. *American Indians in United States History*. Norman: University of Oklahoma Press, 2004.

Nofi, Albert A. *The Spanish-American War, 1898*. Conshohocken, Pa.: Combined Books, 1996.

Northern Mariana Visitors Authority. Available online. URL: http://www.mymarianas.com.

Nugent, Walter. *Habits of Empire: A History of American Expansion*. New York: Alfred A. Knopf, 2008.

O'Brien, Gregory. *The Timeline of Native Americans*. Berkeley, Calif.: Thunder Bay Press, 2008.

The Official Portal for the Island of Guam. Available online. URL: http://www.guam.gov.

Raum, Elizabeth. *The California Gold Rush: An Interactive History Adventure*. Mankato, Minn.: Capstone Press, 2008.

Rogozinski, Jan. *A Brief History of the Caribbean*. New York: Facts On File, 1999.

Schmidt, Thomas and Jeremy. *The Saga of Lewis & Clark: Into the Uncharted West*. New York: DK Publishing, 1999.

Simmons, Marc. *The Santa Fe Trail*. Lawrence: University Press of Kansas, 1986.

Sonneborn, Liz. *The California Gold Rush: Transforming the American West*. New York: Chelsea House Publishers, 2008.

Smith, Gary A. *State and National Boundaries*. Jefferson, N.C.: McFarland & Company, 2004.

Somerlott, Robert. *The Spanish-American War: "Remember the Maine."* Berkeley Heights, N.J.: Enslow Publishers, 2002.

Staten, Clifford L. *The History of Cuba*. New York: Palgrave Macmillan, 2005.

Stein, Mark. *How the States Got Their Shapes*. New York: Harper Paperbacks, 2009.

Stegner, Wallace, and Richard W. Etulain. *Mormon Country*. Lincoln, Neb.: Bison Books, 2003.

Stone, Scott C. S. *Yesterday in Hawaii: A Voyage Through Time*. Waipahu, Hawaii: Island Heritage Press, 2003.

Stuart, Peter C. *Planting the American Flag: Twelve Men Who Expanded the United States Overseas*. Jefferson, N.C.: McFarland & Company, 2007.

Taberosi, Danko, and David T. Vann. *Student Atlas of Guam*. Honolulu, Hawaii: Bess Press, 2007.

Vesser, Cyrus. *A World Safe for Capitalism: Dollar Diplomacy and America's Rise to Global Power*. New York: Columbia University Press, 2002.

Wade, Mary D. *Texas History*. Portsmouth, N.H.: Heinemann Educational Books, 2008.

Waldman, Carl. *Atlas of the North American Indian*. New York: Facts On File, 2009.

Walker, Jane C. *John Tyler: A President of Firsts*. Granville, Ohio: McDonald and Woodward Publishing Company, 2001.

Worth, Richard. *Puerto Rico in American History*. Berkeley Heights, N.J.: Enslow Publishers, 2008.

Index

Page numbers in **boldface** indicate topics covered in depth in the **A** to **Z** section of the book.